PLAY YOUR WAY TO SATISFACTION

Live, laugh, and love your way into the Hall of Fame with Graham Masterton's playbook on playful sex. Almost overnight, you can turn a ho-hum sex life upside down with revealing advice compiled from lovers who have made fun-filled passion their favorite pastime. . . .

Score points with your partner by discovering:

- Why Sexual Play Is So Important
- How to Make Sex Fun Again
- Games People Play
- Sexual Play-acting
- How to Get a Buzz Out of Sex Toys
  And More!

THE
SECRETS
OF SEXUAL
PLAY

Graham Masterton

AN ONYX BOOK

ONYX
Published by New American Library, a division of
Penguin Putnam Inc., 375 Hudson Street,
New York, New York 10014, U.S.A.
Penguin Books Ltd, 27 Wrights Lane,
London W8 5TZ, England
Penguin Books Australia Ltd,
Ringwood, Victoria, Australia
Penguin Books Canada Ltd, 10 Alcorn Avenue,
Toronto, Ontario, Canada M4V 3B2
Penguin Books (N.Z.) Ltd, 182–190 Wairau Road,
Auckland 10, New Zealand

Penguin Books Ltd, Registered Offices:
Hardmondsworth, Middlesex, England

First published by Onyx, an imprint of New American Library,
a division of Penguin Putnam Inc.

First Onyx Printing, November 1999
10   9   8   7   6   5   4   3   2   1

Copyright © Graham Masterton, 1999

All rights reserved

 REGISTERED TRADEMARK—MARCA REGISTRADA

For Laura Anne Gilman, with thanks

1
Come Out to Play

Here's a little game that Veronica, a 34-year-old research assistant from Seattle, Washington, likes to play with her husband, Ted, a 37-year-old marine engineer. "We're still at that stage of our relationship where we make love whenever and wherever we can. In the living room, in the kitchen, in the hallway. We hardly ever make it to the bedroom! We're really so hot for each other. But I know that it's embarrassing for other people if a couple keeps pawing each other in company, so we've devised our own little way of keeping sexually close together, even when we're attending a dinner party.

"I'll go out for the evening without any panties on. I mean, that *alone* is enough to turn Ted into a raging beast! It's all he can do to stop himself from sliding his hand up my skirt. But we behave very primly and properly, even though all we can think about is when we're going to be touching each other again—when we're going to be making love.

"I'll do whatever I can to tease Ted during dinner. He'll drop his napkin and when he bends down under the table to pick it up, I'll open up my legs so that he can see right up my skirt. Once—under cover of a very large linen napkin—I managed to hitch up my skirt and put my hand down between my legs so that I could spread open the lips of my pussy. Ted came up from under the table and I swear he was just about to explode!

"What we do is, halfway through dinner, Ted excuses himself and goes to the bathroom. What nobody at the table knows is that he's carrying a pair of my panties in his pocket. He goes to the bathroom and jerks off into my panties, filling them up with come. Meanwhile, of course, I'm back at the table knowing exactly what he's doing and getting real turned on.

"When he's finished, he hides my panties behind the laundry basket or the stacks of towels or wherever. The risk that I won't be able to find them makes it even more exciting.

"Ted comes out of the bathroom and then I make a visit, too. I put on my panties. The lacy high-cut ones are the best, because the sperm clings to them better. It's all gorgeous and juicy and smells like Ted, and if I'm lucky it's still warm. I like to pull my panties up tight between my legs and massage my pussy around and around with plenty of thick, sticky come. I like watching myself doing it, too, in the bathroom mirror. I don't always reach an orgasm, but I did the first time we tried it, and I've managed it a couple of times since. The orgasm really isn't so important, what's important is walking back to the dinner table with my panties all wet and sticky between my legs, and Ted and I are the only ones who know what's happened. We stay in a state of total excitement all evening and we just can't wait to get home and finish what we've started."

What Veronica and Ted are doing is playing. There is no burden on either of them to use skillful sexual technique. They don't have to worry if what they are doing is physically satisfying or emotionally meaningful. They are simply enjoying the thrill of their mutual sexual attraction, and finding a lighthearted way of arousing each other. At the same time, you'll notice, they take care not to offend or embarrass anybody else around them.

Their playfulness makes for a refreshing change. In the past few years, lovemaking has been afflicted by one of the worst diseases of modern times—it has been taken too seriously. Every time you pick up a magazine or watch a daytime TV show, sex is discussed as if it is a particularly difficult science project, rather than a highly pleasurable expression of affection and regard between two people who like each other and, possibly, even love each other.

3

Graham Masterton

If your lover can't find your G-spot he is as much of a failure as an astronomer who can't instantly locate Omega 2 Eridani. If you don't know the ins and outs of deep genital massage, or how to achieve extended orgasm, or how to "female ejaculate," then you are made to feel as if you have flunked sex—as if sex is as much of a mystery as quantum physics.

I read only recently of a woman who claimed to have found "sexual superhighways" in the brain, a discovery that is going to revolutionize love-making throughout the world. Oh, really? Apart from the fact that it sounded distinctly difficult to come up with any scientific proof for such torrid mental turnpikes, what ordinary couple has the time to redirect their mental processes in order to enhance their sexual fulfilment? For most of us, it's challenging enough trying to find the time to make love at all, in between building a career, bringing up children, improving our golf stroke, and avoiding the rollerskate at the top of the stairs.

I'm very much in favor of new sexual research and the discovery of new sexual techniques (or, as it happens in most cases, the rediscovery and refinement of old sexual techniques). Any practical hints and simple insights that can increase your sexual satisfaction are always welcome. But I am very much opposed to any kind of sexual correctness. Women are entitled to sexual satisfaction be-

4

cause they are equal partners in any kind of sexual encounter and they should have their equal share of all of the pleasure and all of the fun. There's nothing political about it. And if you get a thrill out of doing something "incorrect"—like allowing your lover to tie you to the bed or spank you or even pee all over you—that's nobody's business except your own. If it's fun, and you and your lover like doing it, then do it.

Notice the dreaded word "fun." You'd be amazed how many sexologists wince when you mention fun. They seem to think, as the British historian A. P. Herbert sarcastically put it, "People must not do things for *fun*. We are not here for *fun*. There is no reference to fun in any Act of Parliament."

The trouble is, there are too many people who still believe that sex shouldn't really be enjoyable. There are those who think that God gave us sex to procreate, and that sex for any other purpose is lewd and degrading. There are those who think that sex is slightly shameful and shouldn't be talked about openly. There are those, on both sides, who think that sex is a neverending struggle for social supremacy between men and women. There are those who talk with deep seriousness about holistic lovemaking and aromatherapy and Tantric positions. There are those who never talk while they're making love, never say a word, and never think of taking sex out of the bedroom and into the shower, maybe, or the living room couch, or the backseat of their four wheel drive, even if it's still in the garage.

As far a sex is concerned, it seems as though we've learned everything except how to enjoy it. In the past forty years we've made extraordinary and ever accelerating progress, especially when it comes to freedom of expression. We can openly discuss oral sex and anal sex in our mainstream media, and our men's and women's magazines regularly carry column after column about sexual techniques and sexual problems. Should I make love to my sister-in-law? What's this rash on my vagina? I've fallen for another woman, what should I do?

To that extent, we've largely freed ourselves from our pre-1960s inhibitions. In the late 1960s, when I was first writing about sex, there was a reason for this. Unless they appeared to be deadly serious, and unless they were purported to be written by a doctor, sexually explicit books ran a high risk of incurring criminal prosecution. Sex was still regarded by the establishment as a *medical* subject, and sex books were often categorized under "hygiene." Any discussion of sexual variations had to be disguised as a grim medical treatise, with plenty of warnings about venereal diseases and what would happen to you if you inserted a cucumber anyplace other than in a mixed salad.

With the arrival of the so-called sexual revolution, and the challenges to media repression presented by *Playboy* and *Penthouse* and *Cosmopolitan*, not to mention the appearance in neighborhood theaters of hardcore porn movies like *Deep Throat* and *The Devil in Miss Jones*, sexual discussion became a great deal more open.

It was at this time that books about technique were critically important. Men needed to know about basic female anatomy and how to arouse and satisfy the women in their lives. Women needed to realize that they were not only *capable* of achieving sexual fulfillment, but that they were entitled to it. For the first time, words like "orgasm" and "clitoris" came into common social usage.

Naturally, there was a strong emphasis on the *technical* side of sex. There were Masters & Johnson, with their various cures for frigidity. There was Betty Dodson with her women's sexuality workshop, where naked women lay in a circle on the floor with their legs wide apart and masturbated themselves to orgasm with big vibrators. There was Naura Hayden with her dynamic vitamin drink and her thigh-squeezing method for preventing your lover from "banging" you.

Those researchers and experimenters and commentators—no matter how wacky some of them may have seemed—did tremendous work in bringing human sexuality into the light of day. And if you're interested in improving and developing your sex life, it's obviously in your own and your lover's best interests to have a reasonably comprehensive knowledge of how to do it. How to encourage your lover to give you plenty of foreplay. How to make sure that you get all the clitoral stimulation you need during intercourse. How to make sure that you have two or three or even more orgasms every time. How to bring your lover's penis back to full hardness in the shortest time possible. You'll find answers to these and many other technical questions in many of my previous books.

But you'll find something else, too. You'll find lovers who have not only learned about sex and sexual technique, but who have learned to free themselves of any restraints whatsoever about sex. Lovers who can share their bodies and their minds with complete openness.

"It isn't as easy to achieve a state of complete openness with your lover as you might think," said Kate, 36, a media consultant from New York. "You have to trust him or her implicitly, and believe me, that can be pretty alarming. We're not just talking about sharing a few carefully selected fantasies here, we're talking about sharing *every* fantasy and every sexual thought. And we're also talking about trying sexual acts that once upon a time, I wouldn't have dared to admit that I'd even *thought* about.

"I found it very difficult at first. Everybody has private corners in their mind, especially when it comes to sex. But when I understood that this was *play*, that I was allowed to have a sense of humor about it—that a sense of humor was almost obligatory—I suddenly found it a whole lot easier.

"I'd had this fantasy about dressing up like a cat and licking and sucking my boyfriend's cock. I don't quite know where the fantasy came from. Maybe I got it from that musical *Cats*. But for some reason the idea of it really turned me on. Except that I didn't want to tell him about it. It seemed ridiculous, you know? Almost pathetic. And it would have been, if I'd tried to be serious about it. But I didn't.

"When Paul was sitting on the couch watching TV, I came into the living room on all fours. I was completely naked except for a pair of fluffy fur gloves and a ribbon tied in a bow on top of my head to look like ears, and I'd painted whiskers on my upper lip with eyeliner. I put on a silly, purring voice and crawled up to Paul and said, 'Pussy wants her milk.'

"Paul couldn't believe his eyes. He was laughing like mad, especially when I started to unbuckle his belt and open up his pants. I was giggling too, but I tried to make it a purring giggle. I said, 'Pussy has to have her milk,' and I tugged down his shorts and took his cock out. It was only half hard at first, but then I gave it a lick and rubbed it

9

with my furry glove, and it really started to stiffen. I licked it and sucked it again. I adore that taste of a man's cock, when you first pull it out of his pants, and for the first time ever I told him so. 'Pussy loves the way you taste.'

"He was still laughing, but it was a different kind of laughter. What can I call it? Like, *joyous* laughter. Laughter because I was play-acting, and I was being funny; but laughter, too, because I was making him feel so good.

"I pulled his shorts down even further, and then I burrowed my face down between his legs and started to lick and suck at his balls. Then I ran my tongue all the way up the length of his cock, and again, and again, the way a cat might have licked him. I rubbed him harder, too, with my furry glove, and I squeezed his cock so tight that his veins bulged out and the head of it went purple.

"Juice was starting to run out of the little hole in his cock and I could guess that he was coming close to a climax. That's when I said, 'Pussy's wagging her tail,' and I turned around and showed him my 'tail.' A pink feather boa which I had inserted into my ass.

"He laughed some more, but he said, 'Oh God, you're beautiful. You really are something else. You're the sexiest animal that ever was.'

"I turned back around and took his cock into my mouth, real deep this time, so deep that I almost choked on it. Then I nodded my head up and down and sucked on the shaft until I felt him harden and tighten.

"I looked up for a moment and said, Prrr ... pussy wants her cream now ... and when pussy gets her cream, you pull pussy's tail.'

"He reached around behind me and took hold of the feather boa, circling his finger around and around my asshole where it was pushed in. I gave his cock three or four really long sucks, and then he suddenly said 'Kate—'and filled my mouth up with sperm. I opened my mouth wide so that he could see the sperm on my tongue and dripping down my chin, and I gave a big lascivious lick and a satisfied purr, and that was when he pulled the feather boa out of my ass.

"He didn't realize that there were three or four feet of it up inside me, and kept pulling and pulling, and the sensation was amazing, all these damp, tickly feathers coming out of my anus. I bent forward and took his cock into my mouth again, even though it was going soft. I licked every drop of sperm from his balls and then I sucked him hard in case there was any still left inside his cock. That made him jump, but he didn't try to stop me."

Kate and her lover Paul were simply playing, and the benefits of sexual play in any intimate relationship are enormous. Sexual play allows us to act out some of our most secret sexual fantasies without having to be too committed or too serious about them. Considerable stress and resentment can arise in sexual relationships when one partner or the other harbors a secret desire that he or she feels too embarrassed or ashamed to discuss openly. In its mildest form, it can be seen every Valentine's Day when men give their partners half-cup bras and split-crotch panties and garter belts, which is simply a way of trying to show them that they would like them to forget for just one night that they are wives and mothers, and behave like good-time girls.

But it's incredible how often a gift of erotic underwear is met with annoyance or embarrassment. "What kind of woman do you think I am? You don't seriously expect me to wear this?" To which the answer is, No. I don't *seriously* expect you to wear this. I *playfully* expect you to wear this. I don't think that you're vulgar or whoreish or a woman of easy virtue. But I would like you to play the scarlet woman for me, and regenerate some of that sexual electricity we used to have when we first got together.

Try to remember just a little of the pleasure you used to get from playing as a child, the thrill of pretending to be somebody else—Princess Leia from *Star Wars*, or Wonder Woman. The joy of play is that you can use it to pretend that you're somebody else, and that you exist in a fantasy world where anything and everything is possible. When you apply this to sex, the results can be absolutely stunning. You'll discover a whole new dimension to your love life that you never dreamed possible—*without* having to learn any complicated new techniques or positions, and *without* having to go through any meditation routines or exercises or diets.

If there is a diet involved in sexual play, it's a diet of fun. It's a diet of pleasure without shame, of eroticism without guilt, and a diet that will shape up your sexual relationships while giving you all the satisfaction you crave.

There is only one thing you have to do, and that is to free yourself from all of your sexual inhibitions. And when I say all of them, I mean *all* of them. In sexual play, you can do whatever you've always wanted to, but you have to expect your partner or partners to do what they've always wanted to do, too. You can't expect to tie your lover to the bed and have your wicked way with him without him doing the same to you. Successful sexual play involves sharing and understanding your own and your partner's desires. More than anything else, it involves wholehearted *joining-in.* If your lovers gets a bang out of pretending to be a well-endowed gorilla whose idea of dinner is eating a banana out of your vagina before he makes love to you, don't roll up your eyes and make it obvious that you can't understand how anything like this could possibly turn him on. Join in, and make it fun. Scream and wriggle and moan. Stretch your legs wide apart so that he can lick all around your vulva as he comes to the end of his fruity foreplay. Act like a sex-mad she-gorilla, fighting and scratching and whooping as he thrusts his erection into you.

Sexual play is not only fun, it's extremely therapeutic. It allows you to make love without any worry about doing it right, and it helps to break down the sexual habits and inhibitions that can so often characterize a marriage or a long-term relationship. It's time you stopped making love the way you *always* make love. "I know when Dan feels frisky because he frowns and takes off his glasses," said Marcia, 36, a convenience store manager from Tallahassee, Florida. "The next thing I know, his hand is going to come straying across the bed, almost as if it doesn't belong to him, and start fondling my breasts. He'll go on fondling and tweaking until my nipples are stiff, and then his hand will start on a long, long journey downward, by the scenic route. His fingers dips into my pussy to check that it's wet. You'd think he was cooking a chicken rather than making love. He seems to think that all of this fiddling and stroking is something that a man has to do before he's allowed to put his cock into a woman. Sometimes I wish he'd just jump on top of me like a Hell's Angel and rape me, ready or not. Why doesn't he pull my hair and bite my nipples? Why doesn't he just grab hold of me and shake me and fuck me hard?

"No, never. It's off with the glasses and on with the same little puppet show, every single time."

Marcia's sex life had become crushingly routine, but even women whose lovers are reasonably exciting in bed often have fantasies of trying something new. Just as their lovers do, too. But so many people are afraid of upsetting or offending or even disgusting their partner that they never speak out and suggest that they act out those fantasies for real.

You would think that two people involved in an intimate physical relationship would feel that they could say absolutely anything to each other. "I had three of his children," said Ginnie, 33, from Fort Wayne, Texas. "I washed his clothes, I nursed him when he was sick. I shared his laughter and I shared his tears. And in nine years of marriage I could never pluck up the courage to tell him that I wanted him to go down on me, to kiss my cunt. All my friends said that it was wonderful, and that it was one of the best ways to have an orgasm. But nobody had ever done it to me, and I didn't know how to tell John that I wanted it.

"I don't know what he would have said. He might have done it, but I believe he would have sorely resented the fact that I had been obliged to *ask* him to do it, rather than him doing it spontaneously. Then again, he might not have done it, and considered me some kind of loose disgusting woman no better than a hooker. Or maybe he didn't want to look a fool, with a pubic hair moustache. You couldn't tell with him. He was one of those silent men, you never know what they're thinking. That attracted me when I first met him. He hardly said more than 'yep' or 'nope.' But you can't have a satisfying sex life on 'yep' and 'nope.' You have to be able to talk. You have to be able to *explain*. You have to feel free to say what you want, without the other person thinking badly of you."

When you start a session of sexual play, you have to have rules, just like you do in any game. The first thing you have to decide is whose game it's going to be—yours or your partner's. If its yours, you can do whatever you like to him, and if it's his, then vice versa. If you're in the happy situation where you both like the idea of the game equally, then you won't have any problems. For instance, if you want to play that you're a rubber-clad dominatrix and he wants to play your slave, then everything's going to be fine—so long as you appreciate that he might want you to do things to him that seem kind of extreme to you, and *he* appreciates that you might want to do things to him that go further than anything he might have anticipated. Neela, for example, a 26-year-old secretary from Los Angeles, California, donned elbow-length black latex gloves and a black latex basque that left her breasts bare. She whipped her boyfriend's bare backside with a leather cat-o-nine-tails until it was striped with scarlet. She attached six or seven small bulldog clips to his scrotum, and then used a large, well-lubricated vibrator on him, while rubbing his erect penis with a gloved and lubricated hand. He said, "It was like nothing I'd ever experienced before. I never would have asked her to do it. I felt like my whole being was turned inside out, and I had a climax so intense that I blacked out."

Would she have attempted it—and would he have allowed it—if they hadn't been role-playing, enabling them to "hide" behind fantasy personalities? Neela's answer was "probably not," and her boyfriend's response was "certainly not—I'd never let a girl do anything like that to me before. . . . I was always brought up to think that when it comes to sex, the man is supposed to be in charge." For him, being spanked and "tortured" and anally penetrated with a 10-inch vibrator was "unthinkable." "But that's what made it so exciting . . . the feeling that we were going way beyond the bounds of what we normally do."

Since that time, they've played several other erotic games, usually adopting different names. In a game, with a different name you feel much less inhibited. After all, it's not actually *you* that's doing the spanking, it's Madame Whiplash, or whatever you want to call yourself. And if one or both of you really don't like the game, the simple answer is that you agree never to play it again, and it's forgotten, without nearly so much embarrassment or resentment as if you had performed the same sexual act as "yourself." You're using the same psychological transference as a shy person who puts on a funny voice to tell a joke. When they're speaking as somebody else, they can be witty and outspoken and daring. Yet ask them to say the same things in their natural voice, and they curl up in embarrassment.

It's often the same with sexual games. In costume, under a different name, with a fantasy scenario to play out, an inhibited lover can become amazingly inventive and free of sexual hangups.

Freda, a grade school teacher from Pittsburgh, Pennsylvania, admitted to being very bashful about her appearance. Her husband, Brad, was always paying her compliments about her body, but she never liked undressing in front of him and didn't even like him to see her naked in the shower. "I was overweight at school and I guess that's where my problems began. I never liked to undress in the locker rooms because so many of the other girls had gorgeous figures and used to strut up and down with absolutely nothing on, showing themselves off, while I always wrapped myself up in the biggest towel that I could find.

"I lost weight as I grew older, but I don't think I ever quite got over the idea that I wasn't a very sexy person to look at. My breasts have always been enormous and my tummy's kind of rounded.

I also think my ass is too big. Brad tells me that I'm sexy and perfect and all that, but I'm still not convinced. I'm the one who has to live with the way I look, not him.

"Because of that, I always preferred to make love under the covers, with the lights off. It was okay in the dark, he couldn't see me. But of course that meant that our lovemaking was always kind of furtive and hurried. We never got the full pleasure out of what we were doing. We never got to enjoy each other's bodies. And I mean touching and looking and exploring your lover's body — that's what exciting sex is all about, isn't it?

"When you suggested *play*, I thought, 'Uh-oh, what's this going to be all about? Nude volleyball in the backyard, or something!' But when you came up with Doctors and Nurses, I realized that you understood just what was missing in our sex life, a sense of exploring, like you get when you're young, when you first play Doctors and Nurses. And also a way of really looking at each other sexually."

Men love to look at women's naked bodies. Their sexual responses are much more *visual* than women's. That's why they get such a thrill out of lap-dancing and sexy pictures and porn videos. I know several girls who dance for all-nude revues and they refer to the men who sit in the front row as "the gynecologists." But there is nothing wrong in sexual curiosity. The female vagina will always hold men in thrall, and you can bring a whole new intimacy and excitement to your sex life by encouraging your lover to feast his eyes on you, as closely as he wants, and for as long as he wants.

I still talk to women who complain that they catch their husbands or lovers "staring" while they undress. "You'd think he'd never seen me naked before," said one woman indignantly. And another woman complained about the time she sat down on the toilet to urinate while her lover was washing himself in the tub. "I was trying to talk to him, but he had his eyes fixed between my legs." She didn't seem to think that the sight of her urinating was both interesting and exciting to him.

Brad and Freda devised their own game of Doctors and Nurses. They gave themselves names, too, to distinguish their play-acting selves from their everyday selves. Brad was "Doctor Strong." First of all, he asked Freda to go behind the screen in their bedroom and undress. When she emerged, he told her to lie on the bed. He tied her wrists together and lashed her ankles to the knobs at the foot of the bed so that her thighs were wide apart, and informed her that he was going to give her a thorough physical examination and test her "sexual tolerance."

"Doctor Strong" wore a white coat and had a stethoscope hung around his neck. He even wore black-rimmed glasses, while Brad wore no glasses at all. The sense of clinical scrutiny was heightened by the strong, bright lights that "Doctor Strong" concentrated between Freda's legs, and by the video camera that he focused to give him an extreme close-up of her vagina and anus.

Freda said, "It sounds clinical, but it wasn't at all. It was very erotic. There I was, lying on the bed naked and helpless while the 'doctor' examined me. He opened up my vaginal lips and spread them wide. Then he gently massaged my clitoris while he slipped a finger into my vagina, and then another. On the video, you can actually see my vagina beginning to get wet.

"He went on massaging me while he explored my vagina. He drew his fingers out of me and they were shiny with juice. Then he said he had to do a rectal examination, and he pushed his index finger into my anus. I said, 'No . . . don't do that.' It was very difficult at first. My muscles kept clenching and I really didn't want him to do it. But in the end he managed to push his finger right up, and then a second finger, even though this was really tight, and really churn them around inside of my bottom.

"While he was doing that, he pushed all kinds of different objects into my vagina, saying that he was 'measuring my sexual tolerance.' A big black candle, a zucchini, a flashlight, which made my lips light up pink. An empty champagne bottle. A chocolate bar.

"In the end, 'Doctor Strong' decided that I was suitable for sex. He took off his white coat and climbed onto the bed. His cock was enormous and such an angry red. I don't think I'd ever seen it so big and red—but then, I'd hardly seen it all, because we usually made love in the dark. He made love to me in a way he had never made love to me before, taking his time, touching my breasts, kissing them, kissing my nipples, *looking* at them. It was a game, yes, but he made me realize that I turned him on—me, just the look of me, just as much as a stripper or a girl in a porno movie. I always knew that he liked me. I always knew that he loved me. But now I could see that I turned him on, too. Really turned him on. And don't any women tell me that they don't enjoy the feeling that they're giving a man a big, big bulge in his pants.

"Brad made love to me so fiercely that I had an orgasm even before he'd finished. I tried to stop it but I kept getting these little muscle winces in my vagina and in the end I had to let go. I think I screamed, but I can't remember. I do remember shaking and shaking and my ankles tied to the bed so that I couldn't squeeze my thighs together, which made me shake even more. Brad took his cock out of me, so hard and slippery. I wanted it back inside me, I desperately wanted it back inside me, especially since I was still having aftershocks from my orgasm. But Brad rubbed his cock fast and hard, and said something really obscene. I can't remember what it was, but I had never heard him talk like that before and it turned me on even more. I saw the first drops of sperm flying from his cock and I lifted my head up and opened my mouth as wide as I could, to see if I could catch some of it. His warm sperm spurted all over my breasts and some of it hit my cheek. I tried to lick it but I couldn't reach it, so Brad moved up the bed and knelt right over me, and pushed his cock right into my mouth, still spermy, so that I could suck it. I loved it so much, I could have swallowed it, balls and all.

" 'Just taking your temperature,' he said. Then he took it out and looked at it and said, 'Sorry about this, but you're really hot stuff.' "

In return for his successful "doctoring," Freda tied Brad to the bed and played the part of "Nurse Strict." "I said that I was going to prep him for a serious operation. I washed him all over with a rough facecloth, paying special attention to his cock and his balls. Then I said that I was going to shave him. He didn't believe me until I started snipping his pubic hair with my nail scissors, cutting it really, really short. Then he started screaming, 'You can't do that! What are the guys at the golf club going to say?' And all I said was, 'Tell them how it happened. Tell them the truth. And see if they don't feel as jealous as hell.'

"I still don't think he was convinced, but this

was the game we were playing and the deal was that he could do what he liked to me and I could do what I liked to him. I had always had a fetish about men with no hair around their cocks, ever since I saw a man in one of those nudist magazines. His cock was long and half hard and beautiful—not like so many men who look like they've got a turkey sitting in a nest. So I squirted menthol shaving foam all around Brad's cock and started to shave him . . . and even if he said he didn't like it, you should have seen how hard he was. His cock was like an iron bar that just couldn't be bent.

"I shaved him smooth all around and I even shaved the long hairs on his balls, and around his asshole. When I was finished I rinsed him off and dried him and then I massaged his cock and his balls and his asshole with rose-scented massage oil. His cock looked amazing, naked and stiff and slippery, and I could rub it up and down and play with it to my heart's content. I could *look* at it, for as long as I wanted to, and do what I liked with it, the same way that he had looked and played with me.

"I rubbed his cock against my face and licked it and sucked it. I nuzzled down between his legs and sucked at his balls, and licked at his asshole too. He wasn't complaining now. In fact totally the opposite. He kept saying 'Oh, yes . . . oh, yes . . .' and rearing his hips up and down.

"I climbed onto the bed and lifted up my short black skirt. Underneath I was wearing black lace panties and a black lace garter belt and black stockings. I could swear that Brad groaned out loud when he saw that. But when I pulled those little black panties to one side and he could see that I had shaved myself, too . . .

"I told hold of his cock and rubbed it between my legs, around and around, so that he could feel how soft and wet and hairless I was. Then at last I leaned forward and guided his cock right up into me. I said, 'Don't say a word. Nurse's orders,' and clamped my lips right over his, and pushed my tongue down his throat.

"His cock slid into me, and it felt so fat and long that I actually shuddered. And when it was deep inside me, as far as it could go, I could feel our bare skin pressed together, and that's a sensation I'll never forget. You don't know what sexual closeness is until you've both shaved. Then you think, what have I been missing all these years? I never knew what real sexual contact was, not until I felt this. Brad says he doesn't care if they stare at his cock in the locker room. They can stare all they want. He knows for sure that he's getting much more exciting sex than any of them."

So how did Freda feel about sexual play? "It liberated me. It allowed me to pretend that I was a woman whose body was exciting and arousing; and then I discovered through sexual play that it was true, and that I didn't need to pretend. It gave me confidence. It gave me strength. I played out a role and—lo and behold—it wasn't a role after all, it was me."

This is the benefit of sexual play: *self-discovery*. Role-playing has been used for decades in clinical psychiatry to help people to come to terms with their strengths and weaknesses. It enables us to look at ourselves and to understand our own inhibitions and our own desires. In a sexual relationship, role-playing allows us to throw caution to the wind for a while and enjoy the kind of liberated lovemaking that we've always really wanted from our partners, but were afraid to ask for. The results can be not only therapeutic but devastatingly exciting and erotic; and open up a whole new dimension in our sex lives.

Sexual play is very quickly effective in enhancing our intimate relationships. We're not self-consciously trying to train ourselves to find a "sexual superhighway" in our brains. We're not searching for so-called G-spots and other erogenous zones. We're simply letting ourselves go—giving ourselves permission to indulge our most secret desires without guilt and without any shame at all.

This doesn't mean that we can abandon our sexual responsibilities either to ourselves or to our partners. Whatever game we play, it has to have rules or it isn't a game. But the rules of sexual play are no more than these:

1. That each of you not only *allows* the other to act out whatever sexual scenario you each wish, but actively *participates* in it, no matter how wild or extreme it is. You will never know if you like something if you don't enthusiastically try it.
2. That no physical pain or injury is to be inflicted.
3. That if you enjoyed the game, make sure that your partner knows it. A little praise and a little demonstration of pleasure go a long, long way. But if you don't enjoy it, don't spend the rest of the night telling him how disgusting it was and how much you hated it and what kind of a pervert is he, anyway?

Because rule four is that you don't have to play any particular game a second time if you really don't want to. All the same, you should remember that the whole point of sexual play is to give you both an opportunity to try out those erotic acts that you were always cautious about trying before, in case you or your partner gave a negative response. Sexual play is intended to take the caution out of developing and broadening your love life. It's a way of creating a place outside of your everyday relationship where you can both freely express your sexual desires/urges/fantasies without the fear of criticism or recrimination.

Some couples use a similar technique to deal with ordinary disagreements about finances, child-rearing, and other social problems. They create an imaginary "room" in which they can speak their minds to each other with complete freedom and no holds barred whatsoever; and they use this "room" to get to the heart of any difficulties they may be facing in their relationship. Outside of that "room" the usual niceties apply; but sometimes it's important for people to get things off their chest without inhibition but also without screaming at each other.

In the same way, you can create an imaginary sexual "playroom" in which all the normal strictures of everyday life are suspended, where anything goes: oral sex, anal loving, sex toys, bondage, S&M, wet sex, cross-dressing, mutual masturbation, any kind of erotic activity that takes your imagination.

What you do together in your "playroom" doesn't have to be discussed outside of the "playroom" door, unless you both want to. Some couples find it more exciting if they don't talk about it in their everyday lives, and keep it as a private "place" that they visit only occasionally.

"It's better than going on a second honeymoon," said Elvira, a 28-year-old telesales operator from Houston, Texas. "Jerry and I shut the world outside. We put on some mood music and open a bottle of champagne. And then absolutely anything goes. The next morning we don't talk about it. It's something very, very private which we don't need to put into words. What are you going to say? 'Wasn't it great when I came all over your face?' That makes it sound like something out of a porno movie, but in fact those moments are tender and beautiful, like something out of a dream. And that's the way we want them to stay."

Did she think that her "playroom" sessions had improved her love life?

"It's made our lovemaking much more exciting, because every time we have sex we have these incredible images in our minds of the games we played, and all the amazing things we did to each other. And of course we're looking forward to doing them again."

Far from being childish, sexual play is the most mature and civilized way of exploring your sexuality, and it can take you to levels of pleasure and intimacy that few lovers can even dream about.

Jean, a 27-year-old fashion designer from New York, said, "I was the youngest of four girls and we were all brought up very strictly when it came to sex. My mother seemed to think that God had created sex in order to punish her personally. I became a whole lot more liberated at college, and I slept with a whole lot of boys, but I was still very reserved when it came to making love. One boy produced a dildo when we went to bed together, and I got out of that bed so fast you would have thought it was on fire! I couldn't understand that sex could be fun, as well as passionate. I guess I still felt guilty that I was doing it at all.

"I guess a lot of that changed when I met Matt, who's five years older than me, and much more experienced. Apart from that, he has a wonderful sense of humor. He taught me how to be a more exciting lover by playing games with me. He was Tarzan and I was Jane. He was a Roman emperor and I was his concubine, and we were making love with dozens of people watching us and envying us. He was a shipwrecked sailor washed up naked on the beach, and I was a prim young girl who happened to find him. He has such an imagination, I never know what game he's going to come up with next.

"And he encourages me to play out *my* fantasies, too. Like, I'm the daughter of wealthy businessman, kidnaped by a gangster. He ties me naked onto a bed and blindfolds me and then he does all kinds of things to me. Touches me, smears syrup all over me, pushes things up inside me and makes me guess what they are. A banana or a cucumber or a baseball bat handle. Or I'm a slave girl and I have to serve him with food and drink and bathe him and do whatever he wants. And I mean *whatever*. Once he made me bend right over and touch my toes while he pushed a candle into my asshole and lit it. Then he reached between my legs and started to stroke my clitoris, but I wasn't allowed to move even when the hot wax started dripping on my anus. It dripped two or three times, and then I had an orgasm."

Jean's preferred games suggested that she was sexually submissive. "I guess I am, yes. I'm very assertive and dominant at work. I hold down a good job and I can stand up to any man when it comes to business. But I'll admit that I do get aroused by the idea of being used as a sex object. The trouble is, most men are far too intimidated by my daytime personality to try. I don't even think that Matt would have tried to treat me like a slave unless it had been part of our playtime."

There are countless different ways to enjoy sexual play, from the kind of role-playing that Jean and Matt find so pleasurable, to well-organized games of chance. Some couples play dice to choose what sexual activity they're going to try next, others play cards. Others rely on completely random events. One young wife in Tucson, Arizona, took a bet from her husband that if she didn't pass her driving test at her third attempt she would go without panties until she did. She failed, and her husband took full advantage of it. "Mind you, our sex life was never better. He lifted up my skirt in the kitchen when I was baking, and fucked me while I cut out cookies. Even if I *do* pass, I'm not sure that I'm going back to wearing panties again."

Rhoda, a 31-year-old realtor from Detroit, Michigan, tells me that she and her partner, John, have a set of numbered cards on which they have written thirty different sexual activities—fifteen chosen by her, and fifteen chosen by John. Whenever they feel like an evening of sexual play, they check the Dow Jones index, and pick out the card that corresponds to the last two digits.

"I guess you can say that I'm the only woman who has given her husband oral sex as a direct result of the depressed money market in Southeast Asia," she said. "Mind you, when the economy was looking good, I got to sit on top of him almost every other night. But it really is a whole lot of fun."

Fun. That's the key word—the word that so many people seem to forget about when it comes to sexual relations. Fun can bring back the sparkle of your first days together. Fun can rekindle your sense of sexual daring. Most of all, fun can bring you closer together again, and give you the kind of loving that you really look forward to.

Recent studies have shown that laughter is a great aphrodisiac, which is why girls are so attracted to men with a good sense of humor, and men are attracted to lighthearted girls.

Laughter releases your inhibitions and gives

you a sense of well being and relief. So if you can learn to associate that sense of fun with your sex life, you can improve it almost overnight.

More pleasure, more satisfaction, more excitement—they're all waiting for you. All you have to do is make your play.

•

2
The Sex of Joy

You won't hear many sex experts saying this, but a sparkling sense of humor will light up any sexual relationship. Humor will enable you to enjoy the good times even more, and laugh at the times when things don't always go right.

Sex is a vital part of any intimate relationship, but just because it's vital doesn't mean it has to be deadly serious. In fact your lovemaking will always be improved by being relaxed, smiling, and not worrying too much about anything except giving your partner a really stimulating experience.

It is remarkable how many couples who are lighthearted and fun outside of the bedroom suddenly become reserved and cautious with each other when it comes to sex. Their lovemaking is formalized, repetitious, and very rarely breaks free into a display of erotic spontaneity. In bed, they seem to be unable to show their natural warmth and their real anything-goes personalities, and because of that they find it difficult to achieve the sexual pleasure they deserve.

There are several fundamental reasons for this—not the least of which, believe it or not, is shyness. Yes, even in this day and age, a very large number of men and women are still shy with each other when it comes to sex, even if they've been intimate for years. They're worried that if they suggest anything new, anything different, their partner is going to think that they're dissatisfied. Either that, or they're concerned that if they tell their partner what would *really* turn them on, they'd be met with a turned-up nose and an expression of total revulsion. *You want us to do what?* So they think that they'd better keep their fantasies to themselves, rather than risk a humiliating rebuff.

Just remember, though: A desire that isn't shared is a desire kept secret, and the most fulfilling sexual relationships are those in which there are no secrets. Well, not many, anyhow. Everybody has one or two extreme erotic fantasies that may be impractical or harmful or downright disgusting, and even though there's nothing wrong or perverted in having fantasies like this, it's probably better not to act them out for real.

Sylvia, a 24-year-old hair stylist, had a recurrent fantasy that she was abducted by a group of filthy, trail-dusty cowboys, who stripped her and raped her and forced her to have oral sex with two or three of them at a time, and then branded her right buttock with a Circle W, to prove that she belonged to them, and always would.

"How could I explain a fantasy like that to Ray? He's an accountant. His idea of a fantasy is a secretary with a skirt that's two inches too short. He would never let me give him oral sex without washing his cock beforehand. Flossing it, even. But sometimes I really crave the flavor of a man who hasn't sterilized himself. Sweat and piss and that funky smell between the cheeks of his ass. It's only natural, isn't it? And it turns me on. But Ray just wouldn't get it, so I keep it to myself."

There were ways in which Sylvia could indulge her fantasy, at least partially. She could ambush Ray as soon as he came home from work, and open up his pants before he had time to put down his briefcase. Although they rarely suggest it, most men love being sexually attacked as soon as they put their foot through the door. It makes them feel missed and wanted, and it also gives them the totally primitive pleasure of being sexually rewarded by their mate for all the time they've been out hunting mammoth, or buying cocoa futures, or whatever.

Sylvia could also have her butt tattooed (permanently, or temporarily, according to how she felt about Ray) or have her nipples or her navel pierced and hung with a little silver *R*. Jeanne wrote me from Dallas, Texas, to tell me that she had pierced both lips of her vulva and connected them with a fine silver chain and a tiny silver padlock, to which only her lover Martin had the key. "It's only symbolic. I mean it wouldn't take more than a pair of nail clippers to break the chain if I urgently wanted to fuck another man. But it's like my pledging him my obedience, you know? It's like me showing him that I belong to him, like a slave, or a pet. I know it's not politically correct, but it's only a fantasy and it turns me on."

Another reason that men and women feel sexually inhibited is, surprisingly, the open discussion of sexual techniques and sexual problems in the media. Every woman's magazine you pick up contains some kind of article about improving your love life. Every afternoon TV show contains some riotous discussion about adultery or flirting or how to keep your man happy. There's a new book published every week about how to improve your sexual sensitivity or how to give your man multiple climaxes or how to use yoga to make love for nine hours without stopping.

It's good that we can discuss sex so openly these days. But many books and articles make men and women feel that when it comes to the bedroom they are required to perform some kind of incredible circus act in order to give their partners a really good time—and that something's very wrong with their love life if they can't. One young bride told me that she was worried that she wasn't satisying her husband because in spite of the fact that she had read a sex manual before she got married, she had forgotten the sequence of caresses that she was supposed to use on his penis. She was afraid to touch him at all, in case she got it wrong. "I don't want to hurt him, and I don't want him to feel frustrated, and I guess that more than anything else I don't want him to think that I'm clumsy and inexperienced, you know?"

I don't think she understood that many men love their women to be clumsy and inexperienced. In fact, one of my favorite tips for women who are starting out a new sexual relationship is to make their lover believe that they know almost nothing about sex, and give him the opportunity to mold them and teach them. It's a good way of finding out what a man likes to do best in bed; and also of making him feel masterful. One of the most effective sexual lines in the entire universe for you to say to the man in your life is "I'd really love to suck your cock ... will you show me how?" Hands up if you can think of a single man who would answer that question with "No, thank you. I'm too busy tonight."

Another young woman said that her sex life was being completely spoiled because her boyfriend kept insisting on adopting complicated Kama Sutra sex positions every two or three minutes. "I'm just starting to enjoy him fucking me on my hands and knees when he wants me to roll over onto my back and clamp my legs around his waist. Then he wants to do it sideways, or sitting on the end of the bed, or up against the bedroom wall. I never get anywhere near an orgasm because we're always playing musical chairs."

Yet another was anxious because she was unable to bring her partner to climax with oral sex. "I lick and I suck for what seems like hours and he never comes"—not realizing, of course, that it doesn't matter whether he ejaculates or not. I have never met a man who doesn't thoroughly enjoy oral sex, but I *have* met a great many men who don't find oral stimulation strong enough to bring them to a climax.

One woman was almost driven to distraction by her husband's relentless search for her so-called G-Spot. "He spends so much time with his fingers up my vagina, probing and pushing and squeezing and saying, 'Is that it? Have I touched it now?' It's worse than going to the doctor. I mean, the point is, he takes it so *seriously*. He feels that he can never satisfy me properly unless he give me one of those 'flooding orgasms' the books always talk about. He cooks the same way, always following the recipe book to the letter."

It's important to know about your body and your sexuality and the techniques that you can use to help you to achieve maximum erotic pleasure. But it's also important not to be too serious

39

about them. You should maintain your bicycle properly, but you shouldn't be thinking about *derailleur* gears when you're whizzing down a hill. Concentrate on having fun.

These days good straightforward sexual information isn't difficult to find. Neither is good *non*-straightforward sexual information. Only twenty-five years ago, when I was editing a glossy men's magazine, the only illustrated sexual instruction books we could safely merchandise without fear of legal action were the *Kama Sutra* and *The Perfumed Garden* and an extraordinary book called *A Happier Sex Life* that had photographs of wooden artists' dummies in 238 different coital positions. Very stimulating . . . not!

Our centerfold models weren't allowed to show any pubic hair—not even a *wisp*—let alone girls inserting strawberry suckers into their vaginas or urinating into silver bowls, pictures of which have appeared quite recently in mainstream men's magazines. And our advice columns couldn't mention any of the sexual practices that have now become common topics of discussion in magazines for both sexes—oral and anal sex, homosexuality, group encounters, S&M, and wet sex.

We've come a long way since the so-called "swinging 60s." In fact, the magazines and the books and the videos that are freely available today would have undoubtedly caused international scandal in the late 1960s. Personally, I'm proud of what we managed to achieve with magazines like *Penthouse* and *Penthouse Forum*, both of which I edited in those formative days, as well as the groundbreaking Swedish sex magazine *Private*. We gave a voice to people who had never had the opportunity to talk about outdoor sex or partner-swapping or clothing fetishes or bondage or body piercing. We gave practical help to women who had never achieved orgasm and men who were afflicted with impotence. We weren't always tasteful, but we were helpful and provocative, both at the same time. We ran an article on real-life women in their 20s and 30s who simply hadn't known that they could masturbate, and how to do it. We showed men how they could delay their climaxes to give them literally hours of exciting loving.

I interviewed a 22-year-old woman whose idea of heaven was to go to bed with three or four men all at one time—more if possible—penetrating her vaginally, orally, and anally and finishing up by ejaculating their sperm all over her face. Later the same day I talked to a young wife of exactly the same age who didn't like her husband to see her naked. She always insisted on switching off the lights and wearing a nightdress.

In 1976 I wrote *How to Drive Your Man Wild in Bed*, which was the first how-to book to face up to the fact that women needed to take positive

41

pre-emptive action if their sex lives were radically going to improve.

Jane, 48, a college teacher from Austin, Texas, wrote me, "Your book was the first sex book I ever read, and it changed my life and my marriage. I had never realized before that a woman is empowered to improve and change her own destiny, and that includes her sexual destiny. The idea that a woman could do something sexually to a man without asking his permission . . . that I could flirt with my own husband . . . that I could simply pull back the covers whenever I felt like it and take his cock in my mouth . . . that was *great*. That was revolutionary, at the time, maybe not in some of the more sophisticated places around the world— but where I lived, you might just as well have dropped an atom bomb on us. Suddenly, we were not only enfranchised to fuck, we were given all the information we needed to fuck like angels."

Over the past twenty-five years, sexual freedom for women has improved beyond recognition, and the frankest sexual discussion is open to all of us. But in all social revolutions there comes a time when the battle has been largely won and the time has come to enjoy the spoils of war. Unfortunately, it suits some people's agenda to continue the struggle, including those women who still choose to see themselves as sexual victims, and those sexologists who can still find a new sexual technique that you never knew you couldn't do without.

But in all honesty, if you're reasonably well versed in the basics of sexual intercourse, and you're enthusiastic about giving your partner the very best time of his life, there's very little more that you need to know. You should follow your instincts—do whatever you want to do—and *play*. These days, if there's a sexual variation that you're interested in trying out, you can always check it out in a book or a video. You can also use your imagination. Janie, 26, from Oakland, California, wrote me that when her partner Jeff had broken his ankles and his left wrist in an accident, she had taken advantage of his bedridden condition to give herself "the sexual time of my life."

"He had to lie on his back all the time, he couldn't move, so I came into his bedroom and took off all of my clothes, right in front of him. I made him smell my panties, and there was nothing he could do about it. If they were a little bit wet, because I'd been thinking of what I was going to do to him, I pushed them into his mouth, so that he had to suck them. Then I sat on top of him, slowly scratching him and clawing him all over with my fingernails, and rubbing my pussy against his hips and his thighs. He complained, but he always had a monster hard-on. I sucked his cock and took his balls into my mouth and pretended that I was going to bite them off. He told me to stop it, but his left arm was in plaster and his right arm was in a sling because it was so badly grazed, and there was nothing he could do.

"He was terrified that a nurse was going to come into the room at any moment and catch us. But I think that most nurses would have been broad-minded enough to do a U-turn and come back later.

"I climbed up on the bed with no panties on and tugged my skirt up, right around my waist. Then I took his cock out of his hospital pajamas and hunkered down on top of it so that he could watch it sliding in between the lips of my pussy. His hard red cock, and my hairy bulging pussy lips, and all the juice shining, and that fantastic sucking noise. Then I sank right down on top of him, so that his cock went in all the way, right up to the balls. Like, I was fucking him, and he was helpless. He closed his eyes and groaned and I was sure that he was trying to *will* his cock to go soft, but of course it wouldn't. I kissed him and pushed my tongue down his throat and when I was through with kissing him I gave him love bites all over his neck and kissed his nipples and bit them, too, so that when the doctor came to see him he'd be covered in hickeys.

"He begged me to stop, even though I knew he was loving it. I picked up his walking stick, which was real smooth mahogany with a curled-over handle. I wet the handle with my pussy juice and then I worked the end of it up my asshole, as far as it would go. I had a big hard cock in my pussy and a walking-stick handle up my ass; and the stick itself was right up between my shoulder blades. I took hold of Jeff's right hand and gave him a grip on it and said 'tug it, go on, pull it, as hard as you can, it's right up my ass.'

"That's when he really got into the game. Every time I sat down on his cock, he tugged the walking stick and made me sit up again. It gave him the feeling that he was fucking me just as much as I was fucking him; and it also gave *me* this incredible sensation in my ass. I hadn't realized up until then how sexually sensitive my asshole could be.

"I'm usually a pretty noisy lover. You know, screaming and gasping and all that. But in the hospital I had to stop myself from crying out loud, and that made it all the more exciting. I had an orgasm that hit me like a hammer blow and I gripped hold of Jeff so tight and I felt like I never wanted to let him go. He took out the walking stick and my ass was pretty sore but believe me it was worth it. And it was *fun*."

After two or three similar visits, Jeff gradually learned to relax and to get into the playful spirit of Janie's lovemaking. Sometimes, she said, she didn't actually climb onto him, but would simply sit beside him and slowly masturbate him while she whispered "dirty little stories" into his ear.

"Like, 'How would you like it if you came home

and found me in bed with another woman—a beautiful, big-breasted blonde? And you're watching me through the bedroom door while this blonde kisses my nipples and runs her hands up and down my naked body. I can see you watching and all I do is smile at you. The blonde stretches my thighs wide apart and opens up my pussy lips with her long red fingernails. She slides her fingers into my pussy hole—first one, then two, then three. I'm still watching you and I lick my lips and you can see that I'm really turned on. My pussy's real wet and the blond slowly works her whole hand up inside it, right up the wrist, and she has this little gold charm bracelet that jiggles against my pussy lips.

" 'She flicks my clitoris with the tip of her tongue and it stiffens up. You can't hold back any longer and you take your cock out of your pants and start to rub it. Meanwhile the blonde is licking me faster and faster and her whole hand is churning inside my pussy and I'm gasping with ecstasy. I'm so close to having an orgasm that I can't stop shaking and shuddering.

" 'The blonde takes her hand out before I reach an orgasm. She rolls over onto her back and I sit astride her, so that she can lick my pussy and I can lick hers.' This is the bit that really turns Jeff on. 'I pull apart the blonde's pussy lips as wide as I can, and then I slowly lick her clitoris, and suck at her pussy lips and circle my tongue around and around her little pink asshole. And you're dying to join in, aren't you, Jeff? But you can't—although when the blonde reaches an orgasm and I reach an orgasm, you can't stop yourself from climaxing, too, and you shoot your sperm all over the carpet.'

"Of course by that time Jeff is *so* turned on that he climaxes for real. I love to watch it shoot out like that, it's like a fountain. I like to lick his cock while he's climaxing and that really blows his mind. Once the nurse came into the room and he only just managed to put his cock away in time. But I was sitting next to him with a big smile on my face and a blob of warm sperm running down my chin and dripping into my cleavage."

Janie used sexual playfulness to keep Jeff's spirits up during what, in reality, was a situation that was very far from being a joke. She made sure that the intensity of their sexual relationship never flagged, in spite of Jeff's injuries, and most important of all she continued to make him feel like a man, and a very virile and desirable man at that.

The problems that affect your sex life needn't necessarily be physical. I come across literally scores of cases in which career difficulties or money worries or any one of a dozen different external factors have caused serious hiccups in bed. One woman found it almost impossible to have satisfying sex with her live-in partner because she was being sexually harassed by her boss. She didn't want to report her boss because she was sure that she would lose her job, which was desperately important to her, not just financially, but in terms of her career aspirations. Her partner, not knowing about her anxiety in the workplace, thought that she was becoming "frigid" and almost ended their relationship. Another woman lost interest in sex for almost two years after the sudden death of her sister. Moving is another deeply stressful situation that can have a direct affect on your lovemaking. Even going on vacation can cause problems, because you're in strange surroundings and following an unfamiliar daily routine. Normally, when you're making love, you're all wrapped up in an erotic world of your own, but it only takes one downbeat thought to intrude into that euphoria, and it becomes very difficult to concentrate fully on the joys of sex.

As I was told by Dana, 33, a homemaker from Indianapolis, Indiana, "You'll never believe it, but my marriage was almost wrecked by an amateur play. My husband, George, was away for most of the week on business so I joined a local drama group to give myself something creative to do in the evening. I was chosen to play the female lead in *A Streetcar Named Desire*. I wasn't at all sure that I was good enough but everybody else in the group insisted that I was. You've no idea how I worried over that part. I was sure that I was going to dry up or miss my cue or my dress was going to split or *something* was going to go wrong. The nearer we came to opening night, the tenser I was. When George came home and wanted to make love I just didn't have my heart in it. I couldn't stop thinking about my part. I guess I went through the motions but it wasn't the same, and I have to admit I faked a few orgasms just to get it over with. In the end George asked me straight to my face if there was another man. At first I was shocked, but I could see things from his point of view. He said that ever since I joined the drama group, I seemed to have lost interest in having sex with him, and when I did my mind was someplace else. He was sure that I must have a thing going with my leading man, who was a pretty good-looking guy, even if he did run a drain-cleaning business.

"We had a pretty bad argument about it. I accused him of not trusting me. He accused me of thinking that my hobby was more important than his sexual satisfaction. But in the end I told him how nervous I was about playing Blanche DuBois and that I was sure that I was going to make a fool of myself in front of the whole community.

"George was great about it. He said that I should rehearse at home, with him. Not only that, he expected me to *be* Blanche DuBois, even when we weren't rehearsing. Put on the walk, put on the talk, even in bed. *Especially* in bed. We played at being the characters in the play . . . and I got insights into her character that I had never thought about before. How would Blanche DuBois make love to a man? What would she say to him in bed?

"One evening I pinned up my hair and I dressed up in black fishnet stockings and a black garter belt, and a quarter-cup platform bra that left my nipples exposed. George was already in bed, reading through some reports. So I walked in and tossed all his papers aside and said in my best Blanch DuBois accent, 'I don't want realism. I want magic! Yes, yes, magic! And if that is sinful, let me be damned for it!'

"I gave George magic that night. I really did. I kissed him until he couldn't breathe. I undressed him and clawed his shoulders with my fingernails. I sucked his cock, which I had never done with the light on before. I sat on top of him in those fishnet stockings and I guided his cock up inside me and I fucked him real, real slow. When he tried to fuck me faster I wouldn't let him, and I called him all the names under the sun because we were *playing*. I wasn't Dana and he wasn't George and it wasn't Indianapolis, it was New Orleans.

"I could do things as Blanche DuBois that Dana wouldn't have dared."

Two important points rise out of Dana's experience. One is that you should always try to share your sexual feelings with your partner. If Dana had tried earlier to explain to George *why* she didn't like making love, the tensions between them wouldn't have increased to such an explosive level. So many couples end up arguing (or worse) because one or the other of them didn't feel able to explain what was wrong.

Ruth, 27, a cosmetician from Fort Worth, Texas, said, "Frank is a really great guy. Great looking, terrific body. But he used to be really rough in bed. It was very exciting the first couple of times. But when he moved in with me, I soon realized, you know, that he was *always* going to be rough. He didn't know any other way to make love. He was always picking me up and throwing me down on the bed like I was a Barbie doll and pulling my panties to one side and ramming himself right up inside me before I had a chance to take a breath.

"I hardly ever reached an orgasm with him because he didn't give me the time to warm up. I was just about beginning to feel juicy when he was finished. And the way he acted—as if he was the greatest lover on God's earth, although physically he was probably one of the most ignorant and the most selfish lovers that I'd ever had. Whenever he did do anything to turn me on, I felt like he had suddenly remembered something that he'd read in *Playboy Advisor*, like 'go down on her once in a while' or 'massage her clitoris with your fingers.' But if you know what it's like to have a guy with three days of stubble between your thighs, sucking your clitoris until it hurts and pushing his fingers into your cunt and your asshole without any kind of lubrication . . . well, that was Frank. I ended up with red bristle-burns on the insides of my thighs and my ass so sore I could hardly sit down.

"It's easy to say that I should have dumped him. But even though he was so rough in bed he was always a really great personality, and behaved like a gentleman. And he was a trophy, you know? All of my girlfriends were so jealous, and some of my men friends, too.

"Why didn't I tell him sooner that he was being too rough? You want the frank answer? I didn't want to lose him and I was sure that he would be very, very upset. He would think, like, here I am, thinking that I was the world's most virile lover, and all the time this girl's been hating every minute of it. I couldn't see our relationship surviving an out-and-out confrontation like that. He had too much pride.

"Then one weekend I was talking to a friend of mine and she said that she and her husband had started to videotape their lovemaking. It had been *his* idea, originally, and at first she hadn't wanted to do it. But she said she loved it now. It was really exciting to see herself fucking, and particularly sucking her husband's cock. Not only that, it had improved her husband's sexual technique, like, instantly. These nights he went on for longer, because he didn't want the tape to show him up as a somebody who couldn't last for more than a couple of minutes. And he also gave her a whole lot more foreplay—kissing her breasts and stroking her body and all kinds of stuff like that—because it turned him on when they sat in bed later and played it back.

"On Monday I borrowed a demonstrator video camera from the store where I work, as well as a tripod to set it up on. I took it home that evening and when George came back I showed it to him. He said, 'Great . . . what are we going to do with that?' But when I said 'We can make our own porno movies, can't we?' he couldn't believe his ears. In fact he had an immediate hard-on . . . I could see it sticking up under his pants. I guess a lot of men would like to make sex videos, but they daren't ask their partners to pose. But here I was, actually *suggesting* it, and he couldn't wait.

"We set up the lights and the camera in the bedroom. Well, he did it, mostly. Don't ever deprive a man of the chance to show off his technical expertise. I said that we had to think of some sort of story, we couldn't just film ourselves fucking. I would be lying on the bed reading one of George's muscle magazines and I would look as if the pictures of muscley guys were turning me on. I would slip my hand into my panties and start to rub myself. Then I would take off all of my clothes and masturbate right in front of the camera. George thought this idea was great!

"After I had masturbated myself to an orgasm, I would fall asleep, and then this *real* muscleman would walk in—George, of course. As I lay sleeping on the bed he would come up to me and kiss me, and then he would take off his shorts so that he was naked, with this huge hard-on. He would massage my breasts with his cock and rub it over my face, and I would kiss it without even waking up. Then he would turn around and go down on me, while I slowly sucked his cock. I said that it was important for the camera to see everything that he was doing while he was licking my clitoris, and this was definitely my master move, because he had to use just the *tip* of his tongue while he was licking me, which meant that he wasn't going to suck half of my cunt into his mouth at once, like he usually did.

"After that, it was camera and action! I lay on the bed in my short pink dress, pretending to get turned on by George's bodybuilding magazine. Actually some of the guys in it were pretty sexy. I ran my hand into my panties and started to feel myself. I was juicy already because I was turned on by doing it in front of a video camera. I stroked myself the way I like best, quick little upward strokes, and after a while I took off my panties and opened my legs wide apart, right in front of the camera, and fingered myself really slowly and luxuriously.

"Of course, what George didn't realize was that

I was giving him a lesson on exactly how I liked to be touched. And it was the same for the rest of the video. I made sure that he took his time, caressing my breasts and stroking my thighs and gently licking my clitoris.

"When he climbed on top of me to enter me, I whispered in his ear, 'Do it slow ... do it real slow ... we want to see every last juicy detail, don't we?' And he was good as gold. He slid that big stiff cock into my cunt so slowly that even *I* wanted it quicker. But I was properly turned on now, I was literally glowing, and every stroke of that gorgeous cock brought me nearer and nearer to what I wanted. I could feel his balls banging against me. I could feel every curve of his cock-head, every swollen vein. I wanted to take him as far up inside me as it was humanly possible to go. I wanted him and me to be one inseparable person. And that was when I had my orgasm, and for a moment the whole world went dark, I swear it.

"I don't know if George realized that I had been faking my orgasms before, but he was *so* impressed with this one! He said that I screamed but I don't remember. Anyhow, he thought that he had found a way to give me even better orgasms— 'atom-bomb orgasms' he called them, as if he had invented them himself. 'Real orgasms' would have been a more accurate description, but I didn't tell him that.

"He can still be rough sometimes but I don't

mind an occasional tussle. Most of the time he's working on his new technique, and that suits me fine. We have a lot more fun now, and we bought a video camera of our own so that we can act out all kinds of different sex movies. We did a bondage movie and that was something else—blindfold, handcuffs, everything. And George kept me on the bed for over an hour, tickling me and massaging me and masturbating me, and how can I complain about that?"

Note how Dana managed to introduce sexual play into their relationship without being obvious about what she was doing. She didn't have to pop her fingers and say "*I* know . . . I'll pretend that I'm a wanton courtesan and you pretend that you're Casanova who has accidentally strayed into my boudoir." If you read my previous book *The 7 Secrets of Really Great Sex* you will remember that improving your sex life is all about taking control of your own pleasure, and that is exactly what Dana did, *without* making George feel in any way inadequate. "In fact, when he saw his huge hard-on on the TV screen and how much excitement he was giving me he was really proud of himself. It didn't occur to him for one moment that I was using the video to improve his sexual technique."

Most important, Dana had a sense of fun about what she was doing. In any sexual situation, you should try to be lighthearted, because self-consciousness and seriousness are the two worst enemies of really enjoyable sex. Sex is a way of showing your passion and your emotional commitment, but it's also a way of amusing and entertaining and stimulating each other. Losing your sense of humor is one of the worst things that can happen in your sex life. It's a symptom of many different underlying problems, such as stress, tension, jealously, or mistrust, or some kind of physiological problem, such as impotence or *frigidity*—a word I hate, because it makes a woman sound like an icebox. I prefer to describe it as "temporary loss of sexual interest."

I do not recommend looking for the answers to your sexual problems in books or magazines or daytime TV shows. You are trying to achieve what I call *sexual rejuvenation*—a complete lack of worry or self-consciousness in your sex life, the way it used to be when you were 17 or 18 years old.

You didn't worry about technique then, did you? You didn't think that you might not be kissing his penis properly. You weren't concerned with multiple orgasms or triple ejaculations or exotic positions.

Of course, your hormones were humming in those days and getting laid was end in itself. But remember what fun it was. Remember how playful you were. And for many different reasons, men and women *do* lose their sense of humor, and it can be very, very difficult to get it back again.

Your sexual performance can be dramatically affected by all kinds of apparently unrelated factors. A stressful situation at work, or a temporary financial crisis. Tiredness, or drinking too much. Then all it takes is two or three failed erections, or two or three unreached orgasms, and anybody can be excused for thinking that something is going seriously wrong. Once you start to worry, of course, the fun goes out of your sexual relationship like the sun going behind a cloud. Sex becomes a source of anxiety rather than a source of delight, and anxiety feeds upon itself, making the situation progressively worse. The more you worry about being a good lover, the less you'll enjoy yourself, and the less you'll satisfy your partner.

Later, we'll look at ways in which you can bring the sunshine back into your loving and regain your sense of sexual humor. It's not always easy, but it's a whole lot of fun trying!

Sometimes, however, it can happen that one partner in a relationship is naturally lacking in the humor department. This can cause considerable problems, leaving the more humorous partner feeling embarrassed and rejected, and the less humorous one feeling baffled and inadequate without really understanding why.

Aaron, 33, a magazine journalist from New York, said, "I enjoy an occasional risqué joke. Nothing too blue, you understand. Like the one about the people in Minsk whose milk-cow died. They went to Volgograd to buy a new cow but it was 1,000 roubles. So they went to Pinsk and found a cow that was only 300 roubles. They took it back to Minsk, and it turned out to be a really great cow. It gave them all the milk and butter and cheese they wanted. So they said, 'This is such a great cow, let's see if we can breed it.' They let their bull into the field where the cow was grazing, and the bull got all horny and went straight for the cow. But the cow dodged to one side, and the bull missed. The bull tried again, and the cow dodged to the other side, and he missed again. This went on all day. So, very frustrated, the people of Minsk went to the wisest man in the district and explained what had happened. Before they could finish, he said, 'You bought your cow from Pinsk, yes?' And they said, 'That's amazing! How did you know that?' And the wise man said, 'My wife comes from Pinsk.'

"Okay, it's not much of a joke but I told it one evening when Susan and I were having dinner with friends. Everybody laughed, but she didn't, and as we were going home she was furious. And when I say furious I mean Armageddon. She said that I had degraded myself in front of our friends, and that I had degraded her, and that I was totally disgusting. For all the fuss she made, you would have thought that I had stood up in the middle of dessert and taken out my wing-wang.

"I began to realize that I was having a sexual relationship with a woman who felt that sex was holy—that it was some kind of divine experience that had to be taken completely seriously. No laughing at any time. Now, I'm as devout as the next guy, and I certainly believe that sex is a gift from God. But that doesn't mean that I have to keep a totally straight face whenever I'm making love, and that I mustn't tell any jokes about sex. Somebody once said that making love frivolously is what makes us different from the animals, and I agree with that."

Sheila, a 32-year-old computer salesperson from Orlando, Florida, said that her long-term partner Kevin had turned out to have "hardly any sex drive at all." Their relationship had started off well, with plenty of fun and laughter, and the first few months had been "not madly passionate, maybe, but there was a lot of good sex." As time went on, however, Kevin seemed to lose interest in lovemaking, and devoted evening after evening to the Internet, on the state-of-the-art computer that Sheila had acquired for him.

"I wish I'd never bought it for him," she said. "I spend almost every evening alone in bed watching television, and when Kevin finally comes up to bed he's always too tired to make love. Sometimes he'll say okay, okay, we'll do it in the morning. But in the morning he's always too groggy, and he's not exactly a turn-on to look at. Unshaven, hair sticking up, eyelids stuck together. Leonardo Di Caprio he's not.

"I was always a fun person, you know? I used to love laughing and fooling around. When Kevin and I first got together, we stayed overnight at his parents' house. We were supposed to sleep in separate bedrooms. Well, his family were a little bit *rigid*, you know, when it came to intimate relations between people who weren't married. Anyhow, before I undressed I went along the corridor to Kevin's bedroom to kiss him goodnight. I knocked, but there was no reply, so I went right in.

"His clothes were on the bed and he was already in the bathroom. I called out, 'Kevin?' and he said, 'I'm in the tub.' So I went in and there he was, in a big foamy bubble bath.

"Now, I've said that he doesn't look too good in the morning, but actually he's a pretty handsome guy, and he's got a very athletic body. Wide shoulders, six-pack stomach, terrific muscular thighs. I gave him a kiss and then I asked him if he wanted me to wash his back.

"I soaped his back all over, and rinsed it, and then I reached down into the water and fondled his balls and his cock. I said, 'I'm a mermaid, and look what I've found! A sailor, washed up on the shore, with a hard-on!'

"He said, 'Cut that out, will you? What's going to happen if my mom comes in?'

"I said, 'She'll probably be jealous. Most moms are.'

"He tried to get away from me but his cock was already hard. It was bobbing out of the bubbles like a bright red buoy. I rubbed him a few times and kissed him and blew the bubbles away from his cock, and then I licked his face like an eager puppy. But all he could say was, 'Get off! My mom! What's going to happen if my mom comes in?'

"I said, 'She'll see your big red cock sticking out of the water and then she'll know for sure that you love me.'

"He said, 'Listen, you'd better go. This is getting too crazy for me.'

"But I said, 'No! Look at this incredible hard-on! You don't want to waste it!" And I tugged up this little white miniskirt that I was wearing, and I climbed into the tub. Water and bubbles were splashing onto the floor, but I didn't care about that. All I wanted was Kevin's cock inside me. I was soaking wet. I was wearing these little white panties and they were so wet that I couldn't pull them off, so I dragged them to one side, and reached between my legs with both hands and opened up my cunt as wide as I could.

"I said, 'Come on, sweetheart, your mermaid wants you so much.'

"Kevin was panicking, because he thought that his mother was going to walk into the room at any moment. But at the same time he was panicking because he wanted to fuck me. I rubbed his cock up and down between the lips of my cunt; and at the same time he ran his hands up inside the little pink tube that I was wearing, and squeezed by breasts. I was soaked, all my clothes were soaked, but I didn't care. All I wanted was Kevin's cock. And I was laughing so much that I could hardly breathe.

"I knelt over Kevin's cock and tried to push it up inside me, but the bathwater had washed away all of our juices and so we couldn't get it in. So I poured bath oil all over it, and *then* he could slide it in. All the way up, so that his balls were bouncing against my bottom. We fucked so hard that water slopped onto the bathroom floor. We were both laughing. Kevin reached around me and hiked my skirt even more and poured bath oil between the cheeks of my bottom. Then he pushed his finger up my ass and twisted it around and around, and the feeling was so good that I thought I was going to faint and drown, right there in the bath.

"He fucked me harder and harder. He growled and panted but there was nothing serious about it, he was fucking me for fun. We were both whooping and laughing and if his mother had come into the bathroom I think we would have carried on fucking and told her to go back to Kevin's father, to see if he still had it in him. He reached down with his hands and opened my cunt wider and I pushed myself up against him, closer and closer, and all the time his great big cock was ramming itself up inside my vagina, and my only wish was that it could be bigger, and longer, an enormous cock that almost made me choke. And his balls, they were gorgeous. So big, so heavy, so wrinkly and tight.

"When he climaxed, he almost threw both of us out of the bath. Water slopped all over the floor, but we didn't care. We laughed and frolicked in the bath, and then we climbed out and fucked on the floor, amidst heaps of wet towels.

"I bent over and opened his towel and licked his cock; and then he picked me up and turned me upside-down and buried his face between my legs, with his tongue waggling deep inside my vagina.

"I thought everything was fine, everything was great. But I was wrong. The next morning he came down to breakfast and ate a bowl of Chex and didn't even talk to me, didn't even look me in the eye. On the way home I asked him what was wrong and he said that nothing was wrong, everything was fine. But he was embarrassed that I asked his mother to dry my clothes for me, after our frolic in the bath. 'She must have guessed what we were doing.'

"I couldn't believe it. I told him, 'Of course she guessed what we were doing. What does any young couple who are madly in love with each other do when they're alone?'

"It took me three or four days to get him out of this mood. It was like he enjoyed sex and he enjoyed having fun but he didn't want anybody else to know about it."

Sheila had done her best, but it was time for her to realize that there was something fundamentally wrong with her relationship with Kevin. He enjoyed having sex with her, and as long as nobody else knew about it, he loved playing erotic games. But I strongly suspected that he was ashamed of her. Maybe a little too sexy to bring home to mother? Maybe a little too sassy to introduce to his friends? Kevin seemed immature, lacking in self-confidence, and worst of all, lacking in pride in his sexual partner? My advice to Sheila was to give him an ultimatum: If games on the Internet were more stimulating than games in bed, then he should pack his floppy disk and find someone else. You may play sexually in another "room," where the usual rules of your relationship don't apply. But if that play doesn't effectively enhance your day-to-day togetherness, then it's time to start looking for somebody else who suits you better.

Sexual play usually brings out the best in your partner, and brings you closer together, but sometimes it illuminates the differences between you.

You and your partner should complete the following quiz and see whether sexual play will bring you a much more exciting sex life, or whether you should be thinking again about the man with whom you share your erotic dreams.

3
Are You Playful Tonight?

Here are forty-four questions about sexual play for you and your partner to answer together. They have been prepared with the help of 360 couples between the ages of 19 and 40 who have each professed that their sexual relationship is "very satisfying and very recreational." That doesn't mean that over-50s can't have fun, too! But you should try and answer it as truthfully as possible. A sample of 360 isn't sufficient to give a definitive picture of the sexual satisfaction of the entire nation, but it is enough to give you an idea of how closely you and your partner's ideas of sexual enjoyment correspond.

1. I make a lot of noise when I make love (YES/NO)
2. I prefer to make love with the lights on (YES/NO)

3. I like stripping in front of my partner (YES/NO)

4. I enjoy wearing erotic underwear (YES/NO)

5. I enjoy making love in different rooms (YES/NO)

6. I love having sex in the open air (YES/NO)

7. I love giving my partner oral sex (YES/NO)

8. I wish my partner would give me oral sex more often (YES/NO)

9. I enjoy playing with my partner's sexual parts, even when we're not making love (YES/NO)

10. I try to arouse my partner sexually whenever possible (YES/NO)

11. I have tried or would like to try sexual toys such as dildoes or clitoral stimulators or anal penetrators ("butt plugs") (YES/NO)

12. I have erotic fantasies when I'm making love to my partner (YES/NO)

13. I would like my partner to spank me while we're making love (YES/NO)

14. I would like my partner to talk dirty to me while we're making love (YES/NO)

15. I have fantasies about sexual acts that I feel I can't discuss with my partner (YES/NO)

16. I would like to dress up in a submissive costume while making love (French maid's outfit, rubber dress, slave's bondage straps) (YES/NO)

17. I would like to dress up in a dominant cos-

tume while making love (tight leather
basque, SS uniform, schoolteacher's outfit,
nurse's uniform) (YES/NO)

18. I would love to be tied to a bed so that my
partner could do whatever he/she wanted
to do to me—no restrictions whatsoever!
(YES/NO)

19. I would love to tie my partner to a bed so
that I could do whatever I wanted to
her/him (YES/NO)

20. I like to watch porno videos with my partner
and try to copy what they're doing in the
movie (YES/NO)

21. If I haven't tried it already, I would like to try
anal intercourse (YES/NO)

22. I would like more anal stimulation when
making love (YES/NO)

23. I have a secret sexual fantasy that I would
like to act out with my partner but I'm afraid
that he or she will react in a negative way
(YES/NO)

24. I have a very extreme sexual fantasy that I
would never dare to discuss with my partner. (YES/NO)

25. If I was sure that my sexual partner would
willingly participate in a sexual game, I
would ask him/her to join me (YES/NO)

26. I would be prepared to go out without underwear to arouse my sexual partner (YES/NO)

27. I would be willing to include a third person

of the opposite sex in my lovemaking with my partner (YES/NO)

28. I would be willing to include a third person of the same sex in my lovemaking with my partner (YES/NO)

29. I would enjoy masturbating in front of my partner (YES/NO)

30. I would enjoy shaving my partner's sexual parts (YES/NO)

31. I would like to make a video of my partner and me making love (YES/NO)

32. I wish my partner would tell me what her/his secret sexual fantasies are (YES/NO)

33. I would be aroused by watching my partner make love to somebody of the opposite sex (YES/NO)

34. I would be aroused by watching my partner make love to somebody of the same sex (YES/NO)

35. I would like to go to an orgy where several couples are making love at the same time (YES/NO)

36. I would like to make love in front of an audience (YES/NO)

37. I am aroused by the idea of swapping partners with somebody I have never even met before (YES/NO)

38. I would be prepared to be completely nude all day in order to arouse my partner (YES/NO)

39. I would like to see my partner dressed in fetish clothing, such as black rubber masks and straitjackets (YES/NO)
40. I would enjoy cross-dressing during sex (i.e. the male partner wearing stockings and garter belt) (YES/NO)
41. I would be aroused by openly urinating in front of my partner (YES/NO)
42. I would be aroused by watching my partner openly urinate (YES/NO)
43. I would be prepared to gamble (i.e. draw lots or play cards or throw dice) with my partner to perform any sexual act that he or she chooses (YES/NO)

And for question 44—if you were playing a sexual game with your partner, what would be your preferred character? You can name anybody: a famous person from history, or somebody in the news. A movie or TV star if you like, or a character in a movie or a book or a cartoon. You can even name a character that you've invented for yourself, provided you give a clear idea of that person's sexuality and attributes.

This quiz is not intended to give you a scientific analysis of your sexual personalities. But if you and your partner both answer it as truthfully as possible, it will show you how closely your sexual fantasies coincide. It will reveal whether your partner has been concealing any sexual fantasies from you, and how far he or she is prepared to go to play them out for real. It will also give you an indication of whether he or she is prepared to play out *your* fantasies, too.

Jane, 24, a dancer from Washington D.C., said, "My boyfriend Neville was very keen on the idea of having both me and my sister in bed together. He kept pestering me about it, trying to sound as if he was joking, but all the time making it pretty darn obvious that he would have loved it. I guess that's every man's fantasy, isn't it, having two sisters in bed together, especially if they're twins or lookalikes. My sister Sharon and me both have really good figures, large breasts and very long legs. We inherited those from my mother; she used to be a dancer, too.

"I wasn't too sure about the idea, but when I mentioned it to Sharon she said, 'Why not? Let's give him more than he bargained for.' She liked Neville a whole lot. In fact he had almost dated her instead of me, and so going to bed with him wasn't exactly going to be a *chore*, you know? But she said, 'Let's get a little sexual equality into this deal. We'll agree to go to bed with Neville if Neville and his brother Curtis agree to go to bed with each of us.' Well, I liked Curtis, too. He was about three years younger than Neville and a hotshot hockey player, but he and Neville were very competitive, you know? They were always fighting with each other over girls or money or something or other.

"That night Neville and me were watching TV and I said, 'You know that idea you had . . . about going to bed with Sharon and me. Well, it could be a whole lot of fun, couldn't it?' He looked at me like Christmas had come six months early. He simply couldn't believe it. He called me all the sweet names under the sun and started kissing me and telling me that he was going to take me out and buy me all the beautiful clothes I'd ever wanted. I could tell how excited he was. His cock was so hard that it stuck right out of his shorts. This huge black cock with its beautiful crimson head. I started to rub it slowly and he was saying, 'Oh baby, baby, you make me so happy,' and that's when I said, 'There's one condition.' And I told him that after he had slept with me and Sharon he had to invite Curtis over so that I could have a threesome, too. And then he and Curtis would have to go over to Sharon's place and do the same for her.

"His cock went softer and softer—even though I rubbed it harder and harder. He said, 'There's no way I'm going to share my woman with my own brother! No *way*!' I said, 'Oh . . . I'm supposed to be all excited about sharing my man with my own sister but you can't do the same for me?' He said, 'It's different. You're women.' So I said, 'What's different?' And he said, 'You might suck Curtis's

73

cock or something. You think I could just lie there and watch you doing that? And supposing he sticks it up your ass or something? I'm supposed to enjoy him doing that?'

"I kissed him and said, 'I would. And besides, what do you think I'd feel like, watching your cock going in and out of Sharon's pussy?'

"He still didn't get the point. It was okay if he played out *his* fantasy but *my* fantasy was disgusting. I think a lot of it was plain old male-lion mentality. I can have any lioness I want but watch out any other male who tries to have his way with any of them. I mean, Neville is very liberal in some ways. He has a woman boss and he works with women and he's always courteous to them and treats them completely like equals. But the same didn't apply to his sex life."

You'll be able to see from the number of matching "yesses" and "nos" how closely your partner's sexual attitudes tally with yours. If you match thirty or more yesses then you are both sexually creative and very uninhibited, and your sexual play together will be highly exciting and fulfilling.

If you match twenty-five to thirty then you are very open-minded about sex and there are many opportunities for you to explore new sexual acts and different sexual scenarios. All the same, you do have strictly drawn limits beyond which you are not prepared to venture, at least not yet. In time, when you and your partner have played out some of your less extreme sexual fantasies, you might be tempted to explore further.

If you match twenty to twenty-five then you and your partner show every sign of being sexually compatible, although you could be more adventurous. It's possible that you feel pretty much satisfied with your lovemaking for the time being and that you are not especially feeling the need to try anything wilder. On the other hand, you would do well to compare how many yesses your partner has scored compared to you. Does he or she appear to be very much more open-minded about sexual variations than you are? Or very much less? If he or she has matched ten to twenty yesses with you, it's time for you to think about being a little more imaginative in bed, and to consider playing out one or two of your partner's fantasies. He wants to tie you to the bed? Why not let him? She wants to shave off your pubic hair and give you the sucking of your life? There's no harm in trying it out. If your partner appears to be more inhibited than you, why not gently encourage him or her to play out some of your fantasies and fetishes. People are often surprised how much they enjoy sexual variations once they've overcome their initial inhibitions. "I never would have dreamed of allowing Rick to push his cock up my ass," said Donna, a 24-year-old software salesperson. "But it happened one night, after a company party, and I *loved* it. I'm not saying it didn't make me sore, but after that night I couldn't get enough of it. I still sit in the office and imagine what it's like, having that big, hard cock sliding up between my cheeks. Right up to the balls, all the way in." If you and your partner matched twenty or more it shows that you are both very sexual people and that you are far from prudish. Provided you are both sensitive to each other's feelings, and provided you don't rush into something really extreme, you will blossom into a couple who are both caring and daring.

If you match fifteen or more yesses then there is nothing wrong with your sexual relationship that a little more openness couldn't improve. Try to share your feelings and your fantasies more often. Don't be frightened to tell your partner what you want and what you definitely *don't* want. But on the other hand don't be frightened to be a little more creative when it comes to making love. You'll be truly surprised what a little more flirting can do for your sex life; a few more surreptitious squeezes; a little more ostentatious undressing when you go to bed. Make a point of finding out what kind of women turn your partner on the most, and see what happens when *you* dress and behave the way they do. This doesn't mean changing your sexual self in any way; it simply means *playing* at being sexy. Jim, a 33-year-old aero engineer from Seattle, Washington, came home to find that his partner Moira, a 31-year-old secretary, had been to the hairdresser to have her blonde hair cut in a pixie-style, and was wearing nothing but a see-through baby-doll nightdress. "She'd picked up on something which has always attracted me, which is women with very short hair and very big breasts. I guess it's the contrast turns me on, the boyish hair and the totally womanly boobs. Whatever it is, Moira had caught it exactly. She had really turned herself into my fantasy woman, and I can tell you that I showed her my appreciation with a whole night of making love."

If you match fewer than ten yesses then you and your partner need to do some serious talking about your sexual relationship. Are you both inhibited? Or is one of you so repressed that you can't even consider anything but the most straightforward acts of intercourse? Are you afraid to admit that you have fantasies? Are you afraid that, if you try to act them out with your partner, that he or she may find them perverted or disgusting, and that your relationship will be jeopardized? You need to talk this over, and make a resolution that you'll try to be more open and honest about what you think about sex and what you feel about the love that you've been making together.

When it comes to your sexual relationships, there is no substitute for communicating openly and honestly how you feel and what your needs are. That doesn't necessarily mean *talking*, although talking is always good. Actions can speak just as loudly as words, and if you can't find the words to express what you want, then show your partner through sexual play.

Neville got his big night with Jane and Sharon, although it didn't turn out exactly the way he'd fantasized about it . . . few fantasies ever do.

Jane said, "Sharon came around to our apartment round about nine. Neville had put some smooth blues on the CD player, and lit a few candles so that the whole place looked more romantic. He'd even bought some bottles of champagne. I guess he thought that this was going to the greatest night of his life . . . listening to Isaac Hayes and drinking Moët and fucking two beautiful sisters.

"Sharon looked amazing. She had brushed her hair up into this big bouffant style and she wore a clinging gold dress and gold high-heeled shoes. I'll tell you, she absolutely oozed out sex. We all sat on the couch together and sipped champagne and Neville kept saying how excited he was and how cool and modern and mature we both were, and what a gas we were going to have.

"Neville was only wearing a satin robe and I kept sliding my hand underneath it and feeling his cock, which was just incredibly hard. His cock was huge—at least eight or nine inches—but that night it felt like twice the size. I scratched his balls with my fingernails and he had to push my hand away and ask me to stop because he was getting too excited. But at the same time Sharon was sliding her hand into the top of his robe and caressing his chest and tugging at his nipple-ring. She had her breasts squashed against his arm and she kept licking her lips and fluttering her eyelids and I swear to God I could see steam coming out of his ears.

"I knelt up behind him and licked his neck and kissed him and said, 'You wanted to take us to bed . . . why don't you take us to bed?' He wanted a sexual game and this was it: Sharon and me were playing at being wanton temptresses. So Neville took our hands and led us into the bedroom. There were purple satin sheets on the bed—he'd bought them specially—and there were more candles flickering everywhere. Not only that, there were two vibrators on the nightstand, as well as a strap-on dildo—like a man's cock complete with balls and everything and a harness for women to wear it.

"I picked it up and said, 'What's this, Neville? I never saw this before.' He said, 'I bought it in case you two girls wanted to put on a little show for me.' Well, Sharon and me looked at each other and I think it was then that we knew exactly what were going to do. Like, there was a kind of telepathy between us, you know? The way there always had been all of our lives. And what we were going to do wasn't exactly what Neville was planning to do.

"I was wearing a short red satin robe and I untied the belt and slipped it off my shoulders and let it drop off onto the floor, so that I was naked. Sharon wriggled out of her dress and Neville couldn't take his eyes off her, especially when she had her arms raised and the dress was all caught around her head. She was completely naked underneath, with the same big breasts as me, with stiff black nipples, and her cunt was fully waxed, which mine wasn't. Neville said, 'This is like a dream. I can't believe this is happening to me. This is like a dream.'

"This isn't any dream, honey,' I told him. 'This is real.' I climbed onto the bed and stretched myself out. I licked my lips and then I took both of my breasts in my hands and squeezed them and rolled my nipples between my fingers. Sharon climbed onto the bed, too, and lay beside me. She put her arms around me and kissed me and ran her hands through my hair, and then both of us looked at Neville as if he were intruding.

"We were only playing a game for Neville's benefit, but it was still very sexy. Sharon gave me a full kiss on the lips, and then she took my hands away from my breasts and started to squeeze them and massage them herself. She leaned over me so that her nipples kept brushing against mine, and it was like nothing I'd ever felt before, another woman's nipples touching my nipples, especially my own sister's nipples. I stroked her back, all the way down her spine, and she gave a little shiver to show that she liked it.

"All of this kissing and caressing between two sisters was really getting Neville excited. He knelt on the end of the bed, holding his cock in his hand, and he said, 'Okay . . . which one of you wants me the most?'

"Sharon said, 'Jane's your girlfriend, lover-boy. She should have the privilege.' I could see that Neville was aching to push his cock up inside Sharon's cunt. After all, it was so super-smooth. But Sharon opened up my thighs and parted my cunt with her fingers, stretching it wide, and said, 'Here it is, just waiting for you to fill it up. Look how pink and juicy it is.' After that, of course, there was nothing that Neville could do but shuffle up between my legs. I reached out for him and gave him the dreamiest, most seductive look. It wasn't hard. He's a very handsome man, after all. And what a physique. And that enormous cock sticking up so hard that I could see it beating in time to his heartbeat, and a drop of juice shining at the tip of it because he was so excited.

"Sharon took hold of his cock and pulled it down toward my open cunt. She fitted the head of it right between my lips, and then she said, 'Go on, lover, go in slow.' Neville made this kind of a groaning noise and he slowly pushed his cock into me, as far as it would go, and you don't have any idea how filled-up that made me feel—like I

81

could hardly breathe because I was so crammed with cock.

"Neville started to fuck me, and at the same time Sharon was kissing him and stroking him and tickling him, and he had his fingers up between her legs, playing with her cunt. I can't pretend that I wasn't very, very turned on, because I was. Like I kept feeling spasms in my cunt like mini-orgasms and I couldn't sop myself from talking dirty, like 'Fuck me, fuck me, fill me up with all of your hot white stuff. Fuck me in my ass, fuck me in my mouth. Fuck me everywhere.'

"Sharon said, 'Here . . .' and took Neville's cock out of my cunt. It was shining and slippery and she gave it three or four quick, mischievous rubs. I think Neville thought that she was going to let him fuck *her* now, but instead she told him to roll over onto his back, and she told *me* to sit on top of him, with my back to him, so that he could reach around me and squeeze my breasts while he was fucking me. She guided his cock up between my legs and I sat down slow and careful because that was really one hell of a hard-on and it went up so far that it touched the neck of my womb and made me jump. Neville began to lift me up and down on his cock, his hands clutching my breasts, and I leaned my head back and thought that this must be pretty close to heaven.

"But it got better than that, because Sharon crouched down between my thighs and started to lick my clitoris while Neville was fucking me. She licked all around my cunt lips, too, which were stretched wide open with Neville's cock, and she licked Neville's balls. Behind me I heard him say 'Oh God, that's amazing . . . don't stop doing that, whatever you do.'

"Sharon went back to licking my clitoris. I don't know whether it was the idea of my own sister's tongue licking me, but I could hardly stand the excitement and the total pleasure of it. It was like forbidden and beautiful both at the same time. And Neville's cock was sliding in and out me, and his hands were gripping my breasts so that my nipples stuck out and I wanted it to finish but I couldn't bear for it to finish, I wanted it to last forever.

"Neville can usually last for a half-hour or more, but this time he was sweating and grunting and I knew that he was trying to stop himself from climaxing. But Sharon had different ideas. She reached out for one of the vibrators from the nightstand, and she switched it on and started to push it into Neville's asshole. He was shouting at her to stop. I didn't know whether she was hurting him or whether he was panicking that he was going to come too quick. She forced the vibrator deeper and deeper into his ass until I could feel the vibrations myself, coming right up through his cock. She pushed it in and out, and forced it from side to side, and all this time she was still licking my clitoris, licking it so quick and light it was like a whole flock of butterflies settling on it, thousands of them.

"Neville climaxed and as soon as I heard him shout out I climaxed too. I couldn't keep my balance. I fell forward and clutched Sharon tight and I was shaking and shaking like I was never going to stop shaking for the rest of my life. That was the most devastating orgasm I have ever had; or that I'm ever likely to have. It was the kind of orgasm that makes you feel like you're a different person, if you understand what I mean.

"Neville's cock had slipped out of my cunt when I fell off him, and he had sprayed his sperm all over his own stomach. Sharon knelt next to him and massaged his sperm around and around with her hand and smeared it between his legs and around his balls and rubbed his cock with it. She kissed him and said, 'Come on, lover-boy. There are two of us here remember? What's happened to this big hard dick?' She flopped it from side to side, slapping his thighs with it, and it did stiffen up a little, but not enough.

"She said, 'Here, Jane, let's show him what girls can do.' I was a little tired, I guess, but I was still very aroused, and I wasn't ready for this situation to end yet. Neville was partly right and partly wrong. It wasn't real, but it wasn't a dream. It was like a movie, you know, and we weren't ourselves, we were actors.

"Sharon lay down on the bed next to Neville and opened her legs. Her cunt was absolutely perfect, smooth black outer lips, like a black tulip, and crimson inside, and a hole that was brimming with juice. At first Neville thought that she was inviting him to fuck her, but I was her sister and I knew what she felt like and what she didn't feel like. She reached across and gripped his cock tight, and even rubbed it up and down a few times, but when he tried to roll over toward her she pushed him back.

"I lay between her legs and gently opened her cunt with my fingers. I stuck my tongue out, further and further, until the tip of it touched her clitoris. She ran her hands into my hair and said, 'There . . . that's wonderful . . . that's what being sisters is all about.' I licked her clitoris again and I could feel it growing harder and harder. Then I closed my eyes and dipped my tongue right into the juiciness of her open hole. It was fresh and warm and slippery and it didn't taste like I thought it would. I dipped my tongue in again, deeper this time, curling it up and stiffening it so that I could push it in deeper. I licked and I swallowed, and my mouth was filled up with the sweet taste of cunt. I loved it. It was almost like sweet syrup, you know? I pushed my whole face between her legs and rubbed juice all over my forehead and my cheeks and my chin. My eyelashes were stuck together with my own sister's cunt juice.

"I licked her clitoris quicker and quicker, and at the same time I reached up with both hands and took hold of her big pillowy breasts, and tugged at her nipples. I can remember thinking that we would probably never do this again, ever, and I wanted every moment to last as long as I could make it.

"While I was licking Sharon, Sharon was rubbing Neville's cock, fast and furious, and she must have rubbed it back into full stiffness, because the next thing I knew, Neville was kneeling on the bed behind me. He lifted my hips up, and without any warning at all he pushed his cock deep into my cunt, and started to fuck me as if he hadn't had a fuck for the past ten years.

"He wasn't gentle. He gripped my waist and rammed his cock into my cunt like a piston. But right then it was just what I wanted. I pulled Sharon's cunt-lips as far apart as I could, and licked at her clitoris until her thighs began to tense. I knew she was coming. I could feel it, because she and me, we were part of each other. She suddenly jumped up and down on the bed and grabbed me tight, and at that instant Neville came for a second time, holding me tight so that his last few spurts of sperm would go way up inside me.

"After that, we all kind of collapsed and lay on the bed panting.

"We're still waiting for Neville to make a date for his brother Curtis to come over and return the favor. But I guess we all learned something that night, and Neville most of all. People in fantasies behave any way you want them to, but people in real life always have minds of their own. Also, jealousy can hit you when you least expect it. He never thought that he would be jealous of Sharon, but when I started to lick her cunt, he really needed to fuck me, he really needed to possess me, to show her that I was his."

And her relationship with Sharon? "We're sisters. We were born sisters and nothing can change that. So we made love. There's plenty of worse things that you can do to your sister than give her an orgasm. We don't really talk about it. We were play-acting at the time, and it wasn't really us, it was two wild nymphomaniacs. When the play was over, the wild nymphomaniacs turned back into us."

And her relationship with Neville? "Much more three-dimensional, if you know what I mean. Much more mature. He sees me much more for a person now, rather than a sexy trophy that he can walk around with and show off to his friends. It's like he's tried out his macho fantasy for real and come out the other side of it. I don't honestly think we'll be seeing any more threesomes, although I keep dropping little hints. I think Neville realizes that if he felt jealous about Sharon, he'd feel a hundred times more jealous about Curtis. In general, though, I'd say that we were a whole lot closer . . . like, we can talk much easier, especially about sex."

One reason for Jane's improved sexual communication with Neville is that they acted out their sexual fantasies in front of each other and now they are no longer fantasies but vividly remembered realities. Jane was very shrewd in her assessment of what happens when you act your fantasies out for real. In fantasies, everybody else is merely a figment of your heated imagination and does exactly what you want them to do—but no matter how willing your partner may be to help you act out your deepest sexual urges, he or she will always have a strong sexual personality of his or her own.

When you play out your fantasies, you will find that you are not just indulging a secret desire but making new and possibly unexpected discoveries about your partner's sexuality. You may find that your partner responds much more positively to your fantasy than you thought he would. You may find that he adapts and changes your fantasy into something different and even more exciting. Rita, a 27-year-old travel agent from Boulder, Colorado, had always had a fantasy about making love in the grass, in the open air. While she was out driving during the summer with her partner Gene, 31, they were caught in a torrential rainstorm. Gene parked his sport vehicle by the side of the road and led Rita down to a grassy clearing. He undressed her and they made love naked in the rain. Rita said, "It was everything I ever dreamed of, and more—because Gene had dared to take me outside when it was raining so hard. We slithered all over each other's bodies, and it was so erotic that I can't even describe it. And every now and then, there was a crackle of lightning and a great big boom of thunder, which made it even more exciting."

So sexual play can go very much further than satisfying the erotic desires of the person whose fantasy you have decided to act out—whether it's your partner's fantasy or yours. Sexual play provides a scenario in which you can "explain" your most secret urges, but as the scenario unfolds, you have to accept that your partner may well respond to your urges in ways that you didn't anticipate. Neville didn't expect to find that he would be sexually used by Jane and her sister Sharon, instead of the other way around. He got almost everything he wanted out of the scenario (except, of course, to penetrate Sharon, which Sharon made a point of avoiding). But all the same he discovered that people will always be people and not totally obedient sexual objects—except, perhaps, if that's the sexual role they particularly want to play.

Both of you will always have to make compromises if your sexual play is going to lead to greater physical and emotional closeness and if you are trying to discover more about each other's most secret sexual tastes. Like Fay, 34, a jeweler from Scottsdale, Arizona, whose husband, John, was prepared to wear shackles and chains and leather bondage straps so that she could play at being his dominating mistress—but who drew the line at gags or rubber helmets that restricted his breathing. "Things like that make me panic," he admitted. "I can't even go under the bedcovers to give Fay oral sex without feeling as if I'm going to suffocate."

Instead, John agreed to be blindfolded, and to accept a punishment if he spoke without permission (a crocodile-clip attached to his scrotum). Fay found that compromise sufficiently arousing, and John said, "It was a real turn-on, lying on the bed unable to escape and not being able to see what was going to happen to me next."

As you learn more about yourself and your partner's sexual urges, your sexual play will develop and change to exclude those things that really don't work for either of you; or those things that are a one-time experience only, to be remembered as a way of arousing yourself sometime in the future, but not to be repeated; or those things with which you have grown over-accustomed, and that don't excite you so much any more.

You will find yourself constantly changing and revitalizing your sexual play, introducing new and intriguing variations and taking your relationship forward so that after a while you're no longer self-conscious or inhibited about showing and telling your partner what you'd like to try.

In recent science-fiction dramas like *The X-Files* there have been several stories concerned with couples uploading their personalities into computers, so that they can completely intermingle. The passion to intermingle is what drives us sexually. How many times have you felt the joy of "not knowing where he ended and I began"?

Sexual play can bring you a physical and emotional intermingling of remarkable intensity. To use a science-fiction parallel, it can upload you out of your everyday lives into a zone of total openness—a zone where you can openly show each other who you want to be, who you *need* to be, as well as who you actually are.

Sara, 28, a hotel manager from Jacksonville, Florida, said, "I was brought up very strictly and my parents always made me aware of my responsibilities to my family and myself as a person. So I was always well behaved. I was an A-student at school and I went to college to study catering and hotel management. Everybody thought I was very straitlaced—even my boyfriends. But inside of me

I didn't feel straitlaced at all. I used to see movies about go-go dancers and strippers and I used to think to myself, I'd love to do that. I'd love to get up in front of a whole roomful of men and take off my clothes and get them all so horny they were bursting out of their pants. I saw copies of *Penthouse* and *Hustler,* too. The guests used to leave them in their rooms. I used to pretend that I was disgusted, but I wasn't at all. I tried to imagine what it would be like to pose naked with my legs wide apart and have thousands of men masturbating all over my picture and wishing they could have me for real. I used to daydream about it sometimes and masturbate, although I always used to feel guilty about it afterward, as if I betrayed my parents and my upbringing and done something dirty.

"But I kept on having these fantasies, so I guess you could say that inside my modest exterior there was a raging sexual exhibitionist trying to get out. But I never knew how to express myself when it came to sex. All of my boyfriends were really straight guys, and I was frightened to let them know what was inside of me because I thought they would probably run a mile.

"That doesn't mean to say that I didn't get some good lovemaking. But that's all it was. Good, solid lovemaking. Soft lights, sweet music. Cocktail-lounge lovemaking, that's what I call it. But then I met Bryan. He wasn't an outrageous kind of guy in any way. He worked for one of those swanky realty companies, and I met him at a real estate convention at the hotel. In a lot of ways he was just like me. He looked very straight.

"He took me out three or four times and we got on real well. I wanted to pay him back for all the good times that he'd given me, but I didn't have time to cook him a meal. Instead I asked him if he'd like to come over to the hotel for dinner. We had a great evening but we both drank a little too much so I suggested that instead of driving home he should stay overnight in one of our luxury suites. I had to help out on the front desk for a couple of hours, but I said I'd be up later.

"Around eleven I had this phone call and it was Bryan. He asked me if he was connected to Sara's Call Girl Service. He was in suite 1023 and he wanted a girl. I put on this sultry voice and asked him what kind of girl he was looking for and he said, 'I want a slut. I want a girl who will do absolutely anything.' I said, 'Sure . . . we have a girl like that. How soon do you want her?'

"We were both play-acting, of course. But because we were play-acting we could say what we really felt.

"I finished my work and went up to 1023. In the elevator I took off my panties and put them in my purse. I can remember that my heart was beating hard, and suddenly I didn't feel quite like me anymore. I walked along to the room and knocked and Bryan let me in. He said, 'Are you the girl that Sara sent?' and I said, 'That's right. I hope you can afford me. One hundred dollars for a quickie, three-fifty all night.'

"And what do I get for three-fifty?' he asked me. I went up to him and put my arms around him and kissed him, and then I did the most blatant thing that I had ever done in my life. I took hold of his hand and lifted my skirt and pressed it against my pussy. He stared at me, and for a moment I thought the spell was broken, but I said, 'You ordered up a slut, didn't you? You've got one. My name's Slutella and I'm going to give you the time of your life.'

"I unbuttoned his shirt and pulled it off. Then I unbuckled his belt and tugged down his pants. I swear to you that was the first time I had ever undressed a guy. And it was *exciting*, because look what it was doing to him, he was wearing these little red athletic briefs and his cock was so hard that the head of it was sticking over the waistband. I ran my fingernails down his stomach and then I touched his cock and he shivered.

"I pushed him back onto the bed and finished taking off his pants. He tried to loosen my scarf but I wouldn't let him. I said, 'This is all part of what you pay for.' While he lay back on the bed, I went to the television and tuned in to the adult channel. There was a girl with two men and they were having sex by a pool someplace. There was

94

this raunchy music playing in the background, and I used that to give Bryan a striptease.

"First I dragged off my scarf and twisted it around my wrist. Then I slowly unbuttoned my blouse and revealed my bra. I circled around close to him and said, 'Go on . . . stroke yourself . . . show me how much you want me . . . that's better than applause.' He slowly masturbated himself while I dropped my blouse, and unfastened my bra. It probably wasn't a very professional strip-tease, but I loved doing it, and it sure worked on Bryan. I came up close again and fondled my breasts in front of him. I took ice cubes out the ice bucket on top of the bureau and circled them around my nipples so that they stuck out hard. Bryan tried to reach out and touch my breasts but I danced just out of his reach.

"I turned my back on him, and pulled down the zipper of my skirt. It was a tight white skirt, and I eased it off inch by inch—still with my back to him. I let it drop to the floor. I hesitated for a while. Then I picked up the beat from the music on the television and turned around, dancing, com-pletely naked except for my shoes. I approached the bed and danced a little dance at the end of it. I took the scarf from my wrist and drew it between my legs, backward and forward, tighter and tighter until it was sliding right up between the lips of my pussy. Then I climbed onto the bed and drew the scarf underneath his nose so that he could smell me.

"You're right,' he said. 'You are a slut.'

"We had a fantastic night fucking, and we really *fucked*. There was nothing cocktail lounge about it. We were sweating and gasping and sometimes all you could hear was the squelching of his cock thrusting in and out of my pussy and the moaning and the groaning of the girls on the adult channel. I did things that night that I had never done before because I wasn't me. I was Slutella, and Slutella did anything because she was paid to do anything.

"In the morning, while Bryan was lying on his back asleep, I managed another first. I knelt down beside him and I sucked his soft cock into my mouth, and kept on sucking. He began to wake up, and as he began to wake up, his cock grew larger and larger, until he was almost chocking me. He reached out and stroked my hair and ran his fingers down my back and played with my breasts and after a while he said, 'Come on . . . let me fuck you . . .' but I wouldn't stop sucking him. I kept on licking him and rubbing him with my hand until he fell back on the pillow and I could feel his whole body tightening up.

"He suddenly said, 'Oh, wow,' and shot his come into my mouth, all of it, and I sucked it and swallowed it and licked up every last drop. It tasted strange and kind of dry, but I was proud of myself and I sat up straight and smiled at him and said, 'That's it. That'll be three-fifty, if you don't mind, plus tax.' "

For Sara, a game became a major breakthrough in her sex life. It gave her a way of expressing her natural flirtatiousness and exhibitionism—of letting herself out of the closet, so to speak. She says, "I'm still the picture of respectability in my career and in my social life. But I still let Slutella out to play now and again, and she's the greatest fun."

She and Bryan are still together, and she carries one reminder of the sexual personality that is usually concealed inside of her—a gold ring in her labia. "It's just the kind of jewelry that Slutella would have."

Now that we have seen what intimate play can do for your sex life, let's take a look at ways in which you can learn to be more lighthearted in your personal relationships, and how you can use fun and laughter to heighten your partner's sense of erotic well-being.

4

Play Sexy for Me

These days, the pressures of life can be so great that many young professional couples never have time for any play at all, let alone sexual play. More and more relationships are being defined as TINS (Two Incomes, No Sex). In order to achieve their career ambitions and the style of life that they feel they deserve, an unprecedented number of couples are working almost all of the hours that God gives them, which leaves them far too exhausted to think about anything when they finally manage to get to bed but sleep.

What's more, their adrenaline level runs so high that even when they do have a little free time, they feel the need to take part in all kinds of competitive or energy-consuming activities: tennis, squash, golf, running, and gymnastics. They take their leisure so seriously that it stresses them out almost as much as their work.

Understandably, when they *do* find an hour or two for sex, they tend to bring to the bedroom the same competitive mindset as they do to their work and their sports activities. They are more concerned about their own performance than they are in giving and sharing. Too often, they're thinking "how am I doing?" as if they were tackling a major contract at the office instead of simply relishing the incredible erotic pleasure that two people can give each other without even trying too hard.

Once you've been trained to think in this way it's not at all easy to relax—and I mean *really* relax, and concentrate on nothing but how much sexy fun you're having.

This self-centeredness is one of the major causes of young marrieds waking up one morning to find that the fires have inexplicably gone out and the person lying in bed next to them is—physically, at least—a stranger.

Listen to Sylvia, 31, a legal assistant from Orlando, Florida. She wrote me because she was genuinely baffled by the increasing sexual remoteness in her relationship with her husband of two and a half years, Peter, a 33-year-old executive.

"Peter and I are both very busy people and we knew from the start that we wouldn't have as much quality time together as we would have liked. But we made a conscious decision that we were going to work as hard as possible when we were young and create the kind of lifestyle that we'd always dreamed about. New house, new cars, vacations in the Caribbean. Golf club membership, that kind of thing. Peter always aimed to retire at forty so that we could spend the rest of our lives together, twenty-four hours a day.

"We don't make love as often as I'd like, maybe twice a week if we're lucky. I don't know whether Peter wants to make love more often, but he's never told me that he isn't satisfied.

"We're both good-looking people. I'm not saying that out of vanity. We work very hard to keep ourselves in shape. I go to the gym three times a week and Peter sometimes goes four, or if he doesn't, he plays a hard game of racquetball. We've always been very athletic in bed, and I think you could say that we're sexually creative. We've had sex in the shower, in the kitchen, on the living-room couch. I've been doing exercises for my pelvic floor and I've been working on my orgasms.

"I don't know why but early last summer things began to go wrong between us. It was just a *feeling* at first . . . or, actually, a *lack* of feeling. Peter was making love to me and I was suddenly conscious that it wasn't doing anything for me. In the sense that I wasn't particularly aroused. He went on and on, changing positions and caressing my breasts and stroking my clitoris, but I knew that there wasn't a chance that I was ever going to reach an orgasm. So—yes—I faked it. Peter climaxed a couple of minutes later but I sensed that it was an effort for him.

"After that, we made love less and less often. We didn't exactly make excuses to each other but one or other of us would yawn and say 'I'm so tired, I think I'll go to sleep,' and the other one would say, 'Me too, good idea.' We had a few good nights. We stayed with my sister at her beach house at Clearwater one weekend and we made love passionately for the first time in a long time, and Peter gave me a beautiful, beautiful orgasm. But when we returned to work, the magic seemed to fade and the same routine set in.

"Finally we had to admit that something was wrong with our relationship. We tried some alternative medicine. I took water violet which is supposed to cure you of any reluctance to have intimate contact with your partner. Peter was on a course of clematis, for sexual fantasy without any fulfilment. I can't remember how long we tried it . . . maybe six or seven weeks. But it didn't have any noticeable effect, so we decided that our problem was probably psychological rather than physical.

"We went to a Tantric therapist who taught us all about converting ourselves into Shiva and Shakti; and how to have sexual intercourse in the yogic position so that our identities would blend. Although we could make love for over an hour in that position it didn't change the fact that the thrill seemed to have gone out of it. It was just boring.

"I went to stay with my parents for a week. I missed Peter badly, and when I came back I was so glad to see him. I love him, and I know that he loves me. But we still haven't been able to sort out our sex life."

There's a possibility, of course, that Sylvia and Peter had simply fallen out of physical love with each other. Sadly, it does happen. After the roller coaster of your first infatuation, you begin to realize that your new lover isn't quite as wonderful as you thought he was. His eyes are nearer together than you thought they were. His eyebrows meet in the middle. He has this really irritating laugh. And when he makes love he always makes a grunting noise like a pig snuffling for acorns. It's remarkable how quickly passion can turn to indifference, and how quickly indifference can turn into positive dislike. As Vicky, a 25-year-old graduate student from St. Louis, Missouri, told me, "It took Kevin just four months to change from Hercules into Butthead. Whenever I see him now, I cannot imagine why I found Kevin so sexually attractive."

Of course, almost all couples find that their sexual appetite for each other diminishes with time and familiarity. Two of the prime ingredients of erotic excitement are freshness and surprise. Later on, we'll discuss how long-term sexual partners can blow fresh sparks into a sexual relationship that seems to have smoldered into ashes. But Sylvia and Peter had only been married for two and a half years, and at the beginning of their marriage their love life had been very dynamic, which led me to believe that the cause of their problem lay not in over-familiarity or falling out of love but in their attitude toward sex.

The most striking characteristic about both of them was how driven they were, and how *seriously* they took everything they did. This grim dedication led to them both being very successful at work and highly competitive at sport, but grim dedication has never done much to liven up anybody's sex life.

Another problem was that they were both highly controlling personalities. Now, there is nothing intrinsically wrong in one or other partner temporarily taking control of a sexual relationship. In fact if you read my book *The 7 Secrets of Really Great Sex* you will see that it can sometimes be essential for you to take control of your sex life if your partner is ever going to be the kind of lover you've always wanted, and if your lovemaking is really going to develop into something special.

Sometimes it's necessary for you to use the strength of your personality to make it clear to your lover what your needs are and how he can learn to satisfy them. Almost invariably, the result will be that *he* will get more pleasure and satisfaction out of your lovemaking, too.

But when *both* partners are equally set on taking charge, or if one partner takes charge and the other partner resents it, your sexual relationship can become something of a war zone. I'm not talking about open arguments here. Most of the time, the more assertive partner won't even consciously realize what he or she is doing, and the less assertive partner won't complain about it—not in so many words, although they may make their resentment felt in other ways, such as sulkiness or displays of short temper.

These power struggles are rarely motivated by sexual selfishness. Your lover may physically maneuver you into making love doggy fashion or give your clitoris a furious rubbing because he sincerely believes that you'll find it highly arousing. It's what I call "The Expert Lover Syndrome." He's read *The Playboy Advisor* and he's watched all the how-to videos and he believes that lovemaking can be mastered in the same way as tennis. He's making all the right moves, so you must be totally satisfied.

He sincerely wants to give you the best time possible, but he's never considered that you are a completely individual woman, with your own sexual tastes and your own sexual rhythms, and that you may not like to make love by the book. You may prefer to do things differently, or you may have your own idiosyncratic contribution to make. It's never occurred to him that you might like to sit on top of him for a change, or that you might like him to lie back and do nothing at all but enjoy it while you give him oral sex. Janice, a 29-year-old teacher from Minneapolis, Minnesota, said, "I feel like John never gives me the chance to do what I want to do. I'm not saying he's a bad lover, but once in a while I'd like to make love to *him*. The trouble is, I reach across the bed and start to fondle his cock and his balls, and before I know it he's on top of me, kissing me and fondling my breasts and taking charge. All I wanted to do was lie next to him and play with his cock for a while . . . all I wanted to do was *explore* him, suck his balls and twist his pubic hair around my fingers. But the next thing I know, he's fucking me. How do I explain to him that I didn't want to be fucked? Well, not in such a rush, anyhow. I simply wanted to touch his cock, to feel it stiffen up in my hand, to *look* at it, to stroke it, to lick it, to get to know it. But I've never had the chance."

Philipa, a 27-year-old bank teller from Miami, Florida, said that she bought some bright blue liquid latex. "I wanted to paint a pair of latex shorts onto my boyfriend, and then I wanted him to make love to me with a bright blue rubber-covered cock and a bright blue rubber-covered ass." Unfortunately, when she produced her bottle of latex, her boyfriend didn't like the idea at all.

"We had a terrible argument about it. He said I was weird and what kind of a pervert did I think he was? But I found out later from one of his friends that what really upset him was that I had thought up something sexy and original and that somehow made him feel like he wasn't in control."

Philipa found a playful way out of her problem by painting blue latex pantyhose on herself. "I even had a shiny blue latex cunt." When her boy-friend returned, she met him at the door wearing that and nothing else, and he was so amused and aroused by what she had done that he couldn't feel resentful. "We had sex right there and then, on the floor. You should have seen that big red cock sliding in and out of that bright blue cunt."

Vanessa, a 33-year-old playwright from Buffalo, New York, always considered herself to be "very positive" when it came to sex. "Women may have won their political rights and their social rights, but they still haven't won the right to take a domi-nant role in bed. I've been living with Freddie for five and a half years. He's handsome, and he's a good lover, but a very traditional male. You wouldn't have thought that a man like that and a woman like me would get on together very well, but for some reason we do. He doesn't give a shit about the theater and I need that in my life.

"The only thing is, I began to feel that I wanted to make love to him, instead of it always being the other way around. I wanted to penetrate his body. I wanted to feel him submit to me. I started one Saturday morning after I had read in your book about giving men a climax by massaging their prostrate glands. He was lying there watching TV and I snuggled up next to him and started to rub his cock. He said, "Heyy . . ." but he didn't do anything to stop me. Then, when he was stiff, I wet one finger in my vagina and started to circle it around his asshole. I wet it again, so that it was really slippery, and then I pushed it in. He kind of shifted position, as if he didn't want me to do it, but he didn't directly say no, and so I kept on rubbing his cock and working my finger into his asshole until it was buried in him, right up to the knuckle.

"I could feel his prostate, just about a couple of inches inside his ass, and I began to rotate my finger around and around it. Slowly he relaxed and moved one leg so that the cheeks of his ass were wider apart. I was still holding his cock but I didn't rub it any more. I kept on massaging his prostate and he said, 'That's so good, that's so good . . .' and then with no warning at all I felt his asshole tighten up and warm sperm came literally flooding out of his cock. It felt like pints of it, pouring down his thigh and onto the sheet.

"He said, 'That was amazing . . . where did you learn to do that?' I just said, 'I read about it.'

"But even though it was obvious he enjoyed it

so much, he was very reluctant to let me do it again. Any time my fingertip touched his asshole he changed position so that I couldn't slide it into him. Then one night, after I'd tried it again, he turned me over on my face and poured Oil of Olay between the cheeks of my ass. He opened my cheeks up wide and he pushed his cock into my asshole. It hurt and I asked him to stop but he didn't listen. He pushed harder and harder until his cock was buried in my asshole right up to the balls. It still hurt, but it was exciting, too, and I can't say that I wasn't aroused. He reached underneath me with both hands and he stretched open my vulva as wide as he could, as if he was opening me up to prove that there was nothing that I could hide from him, not even my vagina. He fucked me very, very slowly, deep in my ass, and I knew what he was doing. He was showing me that he was the man and that he did the penetrating if there was any penetrating to be done.

"I lay with my face against the pillow and I lifted my ass to make it easier for him. I wasn't going to fight him the way he was fighting me. Because I relaxed my ass stopped hurting and started to tingle and I wanted him to fill me up, totally fill me up. He fucked me harder and harder and then I climaxed. It took me totally by surprise. I started to shake and my knees collapsed. But Freddie hadn't finished and he kept on fucking my ass faster and faster. His cock was coming right out of me and plunging back in again. My asshole was open wide and I was so wet and messy between my legs that I climaxed again, and again, until I literally thought I was going to die.

"Freddie climaxed, right up my ass. I could actually feel his cock bulging inside me. He had shown me who was boss, or that's what he thought. I crawled forward a little way, so that I could feel his cock sliding out of my ass. Then I turned around and bent my head forward in his lap, and took his cock into my mouth, and sucked it, and squeezed his balls, and smeared my mess all over his thighs. I kissed him then, sticking my tongue right into his mouth, and his cock started to rise up again. But I whispered in his ear, 'You don't own me and I don't own you. But every part of me is yours. Think of that the next time you won't let me into your body.' "

After that, Vanessa said, "Freddie began to understand that just because one person physically penetrates the other, that doesn't make them dominant, and it doesn't make the other person submissive. He's much more relaxed now. He's much more sharing—physically, you know, as well as emotionally. It used to feel like there was some kind of invisible force field between us. Now that's gone, completely vanished. I don't think we have a single inhibition, and sex is so much more fun."

Jim, 24, an insurance agent from Boston, Massachusetts, felt growing resentment about his own partner Marie, a 32-year-old music teacher. "She always says that age never makes a difference. She tells her friends that it doesn't matter. She tells *me* that it doesn't matter. But when we get to bed she always takes charge. She doesn't say so in so many words, but she's the one who decides if and when and where we're going to make love, and she's the one who controls what we're going to do. I try to assert myself. I'm a very strong person. But Marie is a very strong person, too, and I guess she has the advantage of age and experience.

"When I want to make love and she doesn't she turns her back on me and covers her eyes with a black sleeping mask. A couple of times, when she's done that, I've forced my cock up her from behind. She didn't try to fight me off, but she didn't move, either. No response at all. So I guess I've stopped trying to impose my will on her that way.

"On the other hand she often wakes me up in the small hours of the morning by going down on me. I'll be right in the middle of a dream, right, and slowly I become aware of this warm wet tongue licking my cock and circling around my balls. Then she'll open my legs and I can feel the tip of her tongue probing into my asshole, too. It's a fantastic feeling, it never fails to turn me on, but she doesn't seem to understand that I have to get up at six o'clock and that I simply don't have the energy to work all day and make love all night.

"She won't give me a break. After she's sucked me, she always climbs on top of me, and steers my cock into her cunt. She always seems to be wet and ready for it. She rides up and down for what seems like *hours*, with her breasts bouncing. Sometimes I'm so tired I start closing my eyes, but if she thinks I'm flagging she grabs my hands, squashes them against her breasts, and begs me to pull her nipples until they hurt. And if I won't do that she swings her head from side to side. She has very long dark hair and she lashes my face with it.

"Another time I was working late on my computer, putting together a big insurance quotation, and she kept prowling around my desk and ruffling my hair and nibbling my ears. She said, 'Why don't you come to bed and finish that off in the morning?' But I knew that I couldn't—I wouldn't have had the time. She hitched up her little black skirt and rubbed her thighs against my arm, and then she hitched it up even higher so that I could see that she wasn't wearing any panties. You try working out risk factors when there's a warm, fully waxed woman's cunt only about six inches away from you. But I was determined that I was going to do what *I* wanted to do. She wasn't going to control my working schedule as well as my sex life.

"She ran one hand through her hair; and with

the other hand she started to rub herself between her legs. She kept saying, "Yes . . . yes . . . oh, you don't know how this feels, Jim, it feels so good. If only it was your hand.' She slid her finger between her lips and massaged her clitoris, and kept on making these moaning sounds. I wasn't really able to concentrate on what I was doing, but I stared at the computer screen and pretended that I was still hard at work. She wasn't going to win, you know? Not this time.

"I was trying to locate some risk statistics when she said, 'You're always clicking that mouse. Don't you think that you and me click better than any old mouse?' And she picked up the mouse, and opened up her legs, and before I could stop her she had pushed it right up inside her cunt, so that there was nothing but the wire showing. She said, 'There . . . if you want it, you'll have to get it for yourself.'

"I gave in. I gently pulled the mouse out from between her cunt lips, and it was all wet and slippery. Then I took her over to the white leather couch on the other side of the living room. I laid her down with her skirt up around her waist and I knelt on the floor and licked her cunt. At the same time as I was licking she was pulling her cunt lips wide apart and playing with her clitoris and slipping her fingers into herself. We had a fight between my tongue and her fingers.

"I licked all around her cunt, sucking her lips

into my mouth, sucking at her clitoris, poking the tip of my tongue into her pee hole, into her cunt and into her ass. She was gasping and bending her back and thrusting her thighs up at me. I sat up and opened up my pants and she was tugging out my cock before I had a chance to do it myself. I climbed on top of her and pushed my cock into her and she let out a sigh like she hadn't had sex for weeks.

"I fucked her hard. I guess in a way I was trying to get my revenge because she'd interrupted me— because she'd made me do what she wanted. But the harder I fucked her the more she seemed to like it. She didn't reach an orgasm, but when I climaxed she held me close and stroked my hair and said, 'Don't worry . . . what an evening. I have had a mouse in my cunt, and then a man. We can always try again later, can't we?"

In each of these cases, both partners were strong personalities and both of them wanted to control when and how they made love, which inevitably led to conflict. But you can see that one partner is almost always a little more flexible than the other, a little more philosophical, and a little more prepared to compromise. In a sexual relationship, compromise doesn't mean surrendering. Quite the opposite. Compromise means using your imagination and your sense of humor to bring back fun and excitement and a sense of sexual novelty.

Compromise also means being responsive when

113

your partner wants to play sexual games with you, even if, at first you don't really feel like it. If your partner is prepared to be creative and frolicsome, then you should at least do him or her the honor of joining in. Who knows? You'll probably like it.

Take Janice, whose boyfriend objected to her idea of painting him with latex. You'd be surprised how many men resent their partners introducing something new into their sex lives. It's all right if *they* come home with a boxful of sex toys, or order up a whole bunch of porno videos, or buy you split-crotch panties or peephole bras or stockings and garter belts. But if *you* do it, they feel that you're trying not-so-subtly to suggest that they're not quite exciting enough for you, and that your love life needs spicing up with artificial aids. You're questioning his virility.

Janice cleverly managed to deflect her boyfriend's annoyance by using the latex on her own naked body. She knew that he found rubber sexually arousing—and later, once she had soothed his bruised sexual ego, he suggested that she paint him with it, too, which was what she had originally wanted to do. In fact she took control of a sexual relationship in which he still believed that he was in charge by having a sense of humor about it, by having fun, by playing a sexual game. Many women would have said, 'Screw you, if that's the way you feel about it,' and thrown the latex into the trash. But Janice was sensible enough not to take his annoyance to heart, and to use subtlety and playfulness to turn the situation around.

Her advice? "If you do fancy doing something different, but you've got the kind of partner who's kind of prickly about his manliness, then talk about it with him. If he seems to like the idea, make out that he thought of it first; or that he persuaded you to do it, almost against your will. He'll be much more enthusiastic, and you'll both enjoy it more."

Vanessa had a similar problem with Freddie. Even though he must have derived intense pleasure from her anal caresses, it was obvious that he began to worry that he was being "submissive" by allowing himself to be physically penetrated by a woman, while he simply laid back and enjoyed it. He was, after all, rather a straightforward, uncomplicated man—a man who believed that he ought to be active in bed, rather than passive. It would have been perfectly understandable if Vanessa, in return, had resisted his efforts to demonstrate that he was the dominant partner, and refused to allow him to penetrate her anally. The result, however, would have been a sexual standoff.

Vanessa was perceptive enough to realize that if she made a point of responding enthusiastically to his anal lovemaking, she would make his resistance to *her* caresses appear to be even more unreasonable. She emphasized her own strength in their relationship after he had climaxed. She immediately kissed him and gave him oral sex, to show him clearly that she hadn't been dominated, she had *participated*.

"I have to admit that I wasn't really behaving in character," she said. "When he was fucking my ass, I was playing the part of this wanton woman who would allow any man to do anything to her. Because I was playacting, I was more relaxed, and because I was relaxed, I got all the more pleasure out of it. Anal sex is amazing when you're in the mood, but not when you're feeling tense and uncooperative."

Now, Freddie doesn't tighten his buttocks and turn away every time she tries to stimulate him anally, and he has even allowed her to insert a vibrator into his anus during lovemaking.

Jim didn't realize how lucky he was to have a highly active sexual partner like Marie. She was older than him, and he found this somewhat threatening, not only in their everyday social life but in the bedroom, too. It was important for his sexual self-esteem to feel that *he* was in control of their relationship, and he became irritated when Marie showed that she had an erotic agenda of her own.

Sexually, Marie was imaginative, lighthearted and enthusiastic; and it says a great deal for her maturity that she continued to be sexually positive when Jim was so reluctant to drop what he was doing and join in half an hour of stimulating play. Actually, he wasn't as reluctant as he tried to make out. It didn't really take much to drag him away from his PC screen. Neither was he so indignant about her waking him up for sex in the middle of the night. From the way that he described it, it was plain that he enjoyed every minute. He loved it, in fact, and he loved Marie, too, but he wanted to feel like her partner, rather than her plaything.

What he didn't understand was that he could achieve this sexual status by going along with Marie's sexual play instead of trying to resist it. If he resisted it, it made him look as if he were sulking. But if he wholeheartedly joined in, he could assert himself sexually by playing games in which he was the dominant character.

He needed to stop worrying about Marie being older and more experienced, and enjoy the fact that she found him so irresistible. He needed to take their relationship much less seriously, take the plunge, and join in. He hadn't even found it amusing when Marie had pushed his computer mouse into her vagina. Instead, he could have adopted the character of a furious, blustering employer, and insisted that she perform a sexual penance for being so disobedient.

"I think the problem is that I'm lacking in confidence," said Jim. "I was okay with younger girls but Marie is a woman, with strong views and strong opinions and a very healthy sexual appetite. It does take some getting used to. But I'll do my best to lighten up. I know you're right. I know that's the way forward. It's just that I'm a Capricorn, and I'm not naturally a lighthearted person, especially when I don't get my sleep."

When two sexually assertive people get together, they can have quite determined struggles over *when* they're going to make love; and *where;* and what kind of lovemaking it's going to be. It can be done without words. If she doesn't feel like making love, she can make sure that she gets into bed first, wearing a nightgown and heated rollers and settling herself into a book. Or *he* can strip down and join her in the shower, even if she felt like nothing more than washing her hair. Or vice versa.

If he puts her hand up her skirt in the kitchen and suggests that they make love on the butcher block, she can immediately take control by slapping him away and making him feel as if he's nothing more than a dog in heat. If she takes a long time preparing herself for bed, with shining hair and perfume and a sexy nightdress, he can take control by giving her a peck on the cheek, turning over, and going to sleep.

The only way to break out of this sexual arm-wrestling situation is for both of you to learn how to play together—how to stop using your lovemaking as a way of imposing your will, and instead as a way of expressing how you feel about aspects of your relationship that may have nothing to do with sex.

What's the first thing that couples do when they have a fight? One of them goes to sleep on the couch. But why? What bearing does your sleeping together have on your opinion of your husband's drunken behavior at tonight's dinner party? What does sex really have to do with the fact that you've spent too much money on a new dress? When I talk about sexual play, I'm not just talking about erotic fun and games. I'm talking about using your sexual union as a way of sharing each other with total intimacy, and at all times, regardless of any political or domestic arguments, regardless of career problems or money worries or other difficulties you may be facing. I'm talking about making love when you're angry or disappointed or worried or frustrated.

Lovemaking is always the first casualty of any problems in a relationship, whether those problems are sexually related or not. Our first instinct in an argument with the person we love is to pull away, to turn our backs, to refuse to be touched. The last thing we want to do when we're seriously stressed is to have sexual intercourse.

Yet sex can be used to communicate your feelings with a far greater intensity than words, especially if you grow to understand that good sex isn't all about performance. You may not believe it, but it's possible to remain physically close even when you're very angry with each other. Most of the time we argue *because* we're in love, not because we really hate each other. We argue because our partner seems so totally unreasonable, and won't think or behave the way we want them to. We want to control them, especially if we genuinely believe that we're acting in their best interests. Our anger wells up because of their refusal to be controlled.

Later on I'll be describing a sexual game you can play that can help you to overcome serious arguments much more quickly and effectively. I suggested a similar game to Sylvia and Peter as a way of rejuvenating their flagging love life.

Sylvia and Peter hadn't had an out-and-out flare-up (in fact, it might have helped them if they had). But they were both strongly controlling personalities and both felt that they knew better about almost everything in their relationship. Finance, career choices, vacations, diet, decorating the home—even how to make love. The trouble was, they were so busy working and playing competitive sports that they never had a moment to analyze what was going wrong between them. They talked about their sexual problem with friends and therapists, but they rarely seemed to be able to discuss it face-to-face. They agreed that "something" was wrong, "something" was missing, but neither of them could clearly articulate what it was, and apart from seeking outside help, neither of them had any idea how to put it right.

There was no question that they loved each other very much. They had plenty of shared interests and they enjoyed each other's company. But they were always vying with each other, even in bed; and really good sex is always cooperative rather than competitive.

What's more, they took their sex far too seriously. Somebody once said that sex is the most fun you can have without laughing, but I disagree. Sex is much more fun when you *do* laugh. Laughter can work wonders for your sex life by helping you both to relax and enjoy yourselves and not worry too much if every act of intercourse isn't exactly like a sequence out of a Hollywood movie. I shall never know how they tumble over and over without getting themselves wound up in the sheets.

To have a sense of humor, you have to be able to laugh at yourself as well as other people, but neither Sylvia nor Peter could see that there was the slightest hint of self-parody in their sex life.

"Something's wrong, for sure," Peter admitted. "But how can it be my fault? I'm fit, I'm virile, I could make love for hours if I wanted to. I think I have very good sexual technique. I can produce seven satisfied girlfriends to prove it. If Sylvia has been finding it necessary to fake orgasms, then I can only suggest that she isn't a very highly sexed person, or maybe she has some kind of hormone deficiency problem."

What if she were to say that your sexual technique was too rehearsed, too athletic, and didn't seem to be spontaneous?

"How can a man be too athletic in bed? That's like a woman tennis player accusing her opponent of hitting the ball back too hard. Surely the answer isn't for the guy to play badly, but for the girl to improve her game."

You think that making love is like tennis?

"There are similarities, sure. You have two people engaged in a very strenuous physical activity. Both of them are dedicating themselves one hundred and ten percent to the same outcome. In tennis, the object is to win the act. In sex, the object is orgasm.

"I something think that Sylvia's not concentrating, that's all. Whenever I have sex with her, she's thinking about God knows what. Shopping, or legal work, who knows. She's got a great body and great stamina, but I do think that she could sometimes make a positive contribution. You know, once or twice, do something to show that she really loves me."

Such as?

"Well, she never goes down on me, let's put it that way. The guys at work, their wives do it, but not Sylvia. I guess you could call it a bone of contention."

Sylvia protested that she had no aversion to giving Peter oral sex, but he always made it so obvious that he wanted it. "He lies back and runs his hands into my hair and tries to force my head down toward his cock. I'd love to go down on him, but I'm not going to be forced into doing it when *he* wants it. In fact, I'm not going to be forced into doing it at all."

She complained that he was hyperactive in bed. "He's always lifting my legs over his shoulders or rolling me over or trying out some Hindu position that he's memorized from the Temple of Konarak. He goes down on *me* sometimes, and I like that, I really do, but he never does it for long enough. I'm just beginning to feel warm and sexy and he's picking me up and sitting astride a chair.

"He's very athletic, yes; and I loved it when we first went out together. It was fun. But you don't want Barnum & Bailey every time you make love, do you? You want a man who knows how to romance you, how to stimulate you, and how to give you a really great orgasm. I like my lovemaking to be very quiet, very intense, very *cumulative*, so that your sexual excitement gradually builds and builds, without any interruptions, until you know that you're going to have an orgasm and you can't do anything to stop it.

"With Peter, it's like trying to have an orgasm while you're dancing the salsa. You can never concentrate for long enough."

That was the sexual deadlock, and I've quoted it at some length because many, many couples have appealed to me for help with a similar kind of problem. Of course it's a matter of improving your sexual communication, but when "something" goes wrong it isn't easy to find the words to discuss it; and there's a high risk that one of you will feel that you are being criticized for your sexual performance, and take extreme umbrage. It is one of the most crushing criticisms of all, to be told that you are not very good in bed, and so it's not surprising that people take it so seriously.

But the answer for Sylvia and Peter—and maybe the answer for you, too—is to try to see the lighter side of sex, and find out how much fun it can really be.

5
Loving and Laughing

Even a really good sexual relationship can be spiced up by sexual play. Jennie, 25, a teacher from Mankato, Minnesota, told me that she and her 32-year-old lover Tom play a game in which he wears a black leather hood and pretends to be an intruder.

"We have a terrific love life. I guess we make love almost every night of the week. But we just like to play this game for a little extra excitement. I lie in bed, wearing nothing but my nightshirt, when Tom comes bursting into the bedroom in his hood. He's naked except for a black leather thong with metal studs on it. He approaches the bed and drags back the sheets. I scream and try to fight with him. He's so strong that I can punch him and kick him and struggle real hard—just as if he was a real intruder.

"I know it's Tom. I know he wouldn't do anything to hurt me. But he looks real scary in that mask, and he never speaks, even if I beg him to. You wouldn't think that it would frighten you, but it does, in a horror-movie kind of way. I always start laughing, but it's a panicky laugh, you know? I'm never sure what he's going to do to me, and he always gives me the feeling that maybe he's going to go out of control . . . maybe it's going to turn into more than a game.

"He grabs my wrists and he handcuffs me to the top of the bed. I'm still laughing and kicking my legs and telling him to stop but he doesn't say a word. He pulls up my nightshirt, right around my neck, and then he pulls open the zipper that covers his mouth, and sticks out his tongue, and licks my nipples.

"I'm still fighting and screaming at him to stop, but he goes on licking and biting my nipples and squashing my breasts between his fingers. I call him all kinds of filthy names. He likes that. It turns him on. He tugs open his thong and exposes his cock and it's always big and stiff and red. He sits astride my chest and presses my breasts together so that he can slide his cock between them. He actually fucks my cleavage and I can look down and see the head of his cock peeping out from between my breasts.

"Then he sits up and rolls his cock against my face. I try to grab his balls with my teeth, and sometimes I manage it, but he grips my jaw with his hand and makes me let go. Then he pushes his huge stiff cock into my mouth . . . there's nothing I can do to stop him. He forces it right down my throat until I practically choke, and his balls are bouncing against my chin.

"He fucks my mouth, and I know that he's daring me to bite him. Sometimes I do, and he punishes me by twisting my nipples. He loves fucking my mouth like that, especially when I'm struggling . . . but he'd never do it if he wasn't playing the intruder and I wasn't handcuffed to the bed. I wouldn't let him.

"After a while he takes his wet cock out of my mouth and moves down the bed. I start kicking him again and screaming at him to leave me alone. I can't stop laughing, too. I'm almost breathless. But he won't stop. He opens my legs up wide and he grips his cock in his hand and holds it so that only the head of it is inside me. I'm kicking and begging him not to torture me. But that's the way he stays, with only about an inch of cock inside me, and my pussy's crying out for it, I want all of it, right inside me, all seven inches. But he won't— and in the end he has me laughing and writhing around and almost crazy for this cock that I can just about feel between my lips.

"In the end I have to give in. I have to say, 'Fuck me, you bastard! Do whatever you want!' He still won't do it, and I have to come out with all this dirty language. Some of it's real dirty but some of it's just made up, and I don't know how Tom stops himself from laughing. Like, 'You and that jackhammer you call a cock, why don't give my cunt a good pounding?'

"At last he pushes his cock deep into me, as deep as it can possibly go, and I stretch my legs wide and I lift up my tushy because I want him in deeper and deeper. That's a real passionate moment. We don't laugh so much then. But sometimes he pushes his cock in so deep that he makes me quiver, and then I laugh; and once I tried to force two fingers up his asshole while he was fucking me and he said, 'Ow!' because my nails were so sharp, and then both of us broke up laughing so much we had to stop, intruder scenario or not.

"We play a few other games, too. Like sometimes I'll wear panties when I go out and sometimes I won't, and he has to guess if I'm wearing them or not—and, if I am, what color they are. You should see him trying to maneuver me into a corner so that he can slip his hand up my skirt, or bending over to tie his shoelace so that he can take a peek between my legs.

"We started the intruder game because I told him I had a fantasy about being helpless on a bed while an anonymous man had his way with me. I tell Tom just about everything, and I think he tells me just about everything, too. If he said that he wanted me to cover myself in ice cream so that he could lick it off, I'd do that. If he wanted me to push a cucumber up my cunt . . . why not, it's only in fun.

"The only thing that would make me uneasy is if he wanted to try something weird and I thought he was totally serious about it. Like he caught me on the toilet one time while I was having a pee and he put his hand between my legs and splashed it all about. I was screaming and laughing and I thought it was sexy, too. But if I thought he was heavily into that kind of thing . . . if he had a fetish . . . well, I love being passionate, and I know when to stop laughing and show Tom that I love him to death. But I think that the best sex is fun sex, because when you're laughing you're *sharing*, do you know what I mean? You're not keeping all these secret feelings to yourself."

Jennie put her finger on the "something" that was causing Sylvia and Peter such problems. They weren't laughing and they weren't sharing. There was no doubt that they loved each other, but when it actually came to making love they were too serious and self-conscious about their performance. Both of them believed that they knew the "right" way to make love, and both of them believed that they knew better than the other. They needed to forget about the technicalities of making love—forget about being a gold medallist in the Sexual Olympics—and devote themselves wholeheartedly to each other's erotic pleasure.

As I've said before, it's important to know about sex and sexual techniques. But it's even more important to lose yourself completely when you're making love—to forget about your inhibitions and give your partner every pleasure that you can think of, and more. Stop worrying about the way you look and whether you're doing it exactly right. Forget about the *Kama Sutra* and the thirty sexual positions of Chinese antiquity, such as "Chicken And Mouse In One Hole" and "Reversed Flying Ducks." Nobody was ever seriously expected to attempt any of those positions, not for real; they were described and illustrated mainly to turn people on.

I'm not saying there's any harm in trying to make love bent over backward, for the fun of it, but most of the more exotic positions are so uncomfortable that you're more concerned about dislocating your hip than having an orgasm. For God's sake don't attempt "Wailing Monkey Embracing a Tree"— not unless you and your partner want to end up in the ER.

Similarly, you can forget about hunting for G-spots and connecting yourself to the erotic super-highway and how to hold a man's penis properly. Most of your sexual technique will come to you naturally, and if you can't remember what you read in my last book about giving your lover a deep perineal massage just before he reaches his climax, then honestly, don't worry about it. You can always try it next time.

Sylvia and Peter had to change their attitude toward their lovemaking. They had to stop thinking that the rewards of sex, like work or sport, were performance-related. They weren't going to lose a game if they couldn't quite hit the 3–5–7–9 rhythm, and they wouldn't miss out on a lucrative account if they didn't always achieve simultaneous orgasm. And neither of them was going to be accused of slacking if they relaxed for a while and enjoyed a simple ministration of sexual loving from their partner, such as kissing, or stroking, or licking.

Many men find it almost impossible to lie back and accept sexual caresses from their partner without actively responding. They always seem to feel that they have to be doing something to arouse their partner in return. They don't seem to realize that women enjoy exploring their lovers' bodies at their own pace, uninterrupted. They find it both arousing and educational . . . watching what makes his penis rise and what makes it sink.

Kelly, a 26-year-old gym assistant, said, "I'm crazy about Greg and I really go for his body. He's been weight-training since he was sixteen and he has such beautifully developed muscles. Sometimes I feel like kissing him all over—you know, just stroking him and licking him and enjoying him. He's been sunbathing so his skin is this light

mahogany color. He's also completely shaved . . .
he has no body hair at all, so you can imagine how
sexy his cock and balls are, totally bare and clean. I
love kissing his cock and licking all around it, and
sucking his balls. He gets these immense hard-ons
that look even bigger because he doesn't have any
hair. But the trouble is that as soon as I start turning him on he starts to caress me back. I'm lying
next to him sucking his cock and he keeps running
his hands through my hair and sliding his finger
down my back and in between the cheeks of my
ass. Or else he starts playing with my breasts and
tugging my nipples. It's not that I don't like him
doing it, but I don't want him to do it *then*, while
I'm trying to concentrate on doing something to
him. If I'm sucking his cock, that's enough excitement for me, I don't need him to keep touching me
and stroking me all the time. It makes me feel like
I'm not in charge of what I'm doing . . . that I can't
do anything in bed without him taking over."

It was essential for Peter to switch off his competitive instincts once in a while and force himself to be sexually passive. He had to stop thinking
of sex as a game of tennis with Sylvia as his
weaker opponent. He had to stop regarding her as
an opponent at all—but as a lover who wanted to
arouse him and give him as much as sexual satisfaction as possible. If he were less competitive
about sex, he would find that Sylvia could give

him more pleasure than he would have thought possible, and then some.

Sylvia had to learn to stop criticizing Peter's sexual gymnastics and realize that, for one thing, he had probably watched too many porno movies and was under the mistaken impression that this was what good lovers did; and also that she wasn't letting him know when she was beginning to become deeply aroused, and so he was changing position to see if could elicit more response. Like many women, Sylvia could enjoy sexual stimulation in stillness and silence, and like many men, Peter took this seeming lack of response to mean that she wasn't turned on at all.

So many men complain to me that "when we make love, my wife just lies there" without understanding that behind those closed eyes, behind that apparent passivity, she is enjoying a deeply arousing sexual experience.

Gina, a 31-year-old prostitute from Los Angeles told me, "I always pant and gasp and cry out and say, 'That's wonderful . . . do it to me . . . that feels so good . . . fuck me, fuck me . . . you're doing it just the way I like it, lover boy,' all that stuff. And men just love it, because they don't get any of that with their wives. They get 'I love you,' if they're lucky. Most of the time they don't get nothing. But the fact of the matter is that when I make love to a man I really care for, I don't say nothing, either. Like it's too distracting. I just want to feel that we're one person, do you know what I mean, all melted together? But if I start to shout out 'fuck me, fuck me,' that's two people having intercourse, that's all."

All the same, it *does* help if you can give your lover at least some indication that you like what he's doing. A little panting, a little gasping, a little moan of 'Ooh, that's *good.*' It will not only help him to learn how to make love to you the way you really enjoy it, but it will excite him, too. It will make him feel like a better lover, and a man who *feels* like a better lover usually is.

In order to help Sylvia and Peter change their sexual attitudes, I recommended some exercises to bring a sense of playfulness back into their relationship. These exercises were not specifically tailored for them. I devised them to help any couple who feels that their sex life has become too serious, too humdrum, and that all the fizz has gone flat. Like Sylvia and Peter, many couples don't really understand *why* they seem to have lost that extra-special intimacy. When they were in bed together, they used to feel as if they were the only two people on the planet. Now they just feel like two people in bed together.

The secret of sexual play is to give yourself permission to break out of your everyday routine and do something quite different—even perverse. Sexual games have rules, but they needn't be the same rules by which you normally live your life.

You need to ask yourself "Why do I always do this?" "Why do I always feel like that?" "What do I need out of my life, that I don't have now?" and "What does my lover need out of *his* life, that he doesn't have now"?

Most of all, you have to ask yourself, "If I could dramatically change my sex life overnight, how would I change it?"

Make up a list of five realistic answers to that question, such as:

1. I would make sure that my lover and I had sex every morning before breakfast.
2. I would wear sexy clothes and seduce my lover as soon as he came home from work.
3. I would sexually stimulate my lover whenever and wherever I could ... even in the supermarket!
4. I would insist on going away to a hotel for the weekend, and never getting out of bed.
5. I would actively encourage my lover to try things that he might have been too reserved to try before, such as anal sex and wet sex.

Then make up a list of five fantasy answers to that question, such as:

1. I would like my lover to tie me to the bed and make love to me.

2. I would like my lover and I to star in a porno movie.
3. I would like my lover to be my sex slave for a day.
4. I would like to make love to two men at once.
5. I would like to make love to another woman while my lover watched.

Whatever you write in your list will give you an idea of what sexual games you can play. Your lover should write his own list, and between you, you should be able to come up with enough playful ideas to give your love life the jump-start it needs. You don't necessarily have to compare lists—you can keep them secret from each other if you want to. They're only a guide to help you decide what you're going to do to rejuvenate your sexual relationship.

Sex Tease Games: These are brilliant for breaking down any sexual reserve or inhibition that your partner may have. He won't be able to stay serious when you try out your teasing games on him, and he won't be able to think about anything except making love to you, which is the whole point of the exercise.

Start teasing him sexually by not letting him alone. When he wakes in the morning, slip your hand into his pajamas and start fondling him. If he protests, jump on top of him naked and start snapping at his penis like a frantic poodle, nipping it with your teeth. Then take it into your mouth and suck him. Wait until he's fully erect and then rub his penis a few times and just bounce out of bed and go to make coffee . . . leaving him in mid-air, so to speak. Your aim is to *tease*, to keep stimulating him until he's absolutely straining at the leash to make love to you.

What makes teasing so important is that you are reintroducing the idea that you can have sex at any time of the night or day. Most couples in a long-term relationship settle down to having sex at fairly regular times: in the evening, when they go to bed, or on weekend mornings. Teasing deregulates sex, returning it to the way it used to be when you first got together. There's no law against having sex at 11:30 in the morning, after all. You see what I mean by breaking out of your everyday routine?

Don't stop at that waking-up tease. When he gets into the shower, get in with him, and make sure that you give him a soaping between the legs that he'll remember for the rest of the day. Take a handful of soap and masturbate him quite hard, rubbing yourself up against him . . . but then suddenly remember that you've left the bacon under the grill, and leave him on the brink.

He may become so aroused that your teasing leads to full sexual intercourse. Angie, a 34-year-old riding teacher from Richmond, Virginia, tried following her husband, Vince, into the shower one morning. "Mostly, Vince is like a zombie in the morning. He can't even speak. But I took your advice and followed him into the shower, completely naked. I'd done something else, too, which really woke him up, and that was to shave my pussy. He was always hinting that he would really like it if I did, but I guess you could say that I was always kind of conservative, and that seemed a little, well, I don't know, *brazen*. But I mentioned it to a couple of my friends, and they seemed almost shocked that I still had hair down there. One of them had been shaving ever since she was fourteen and the other one had a bikini wax every time she had her nails done. But anyhow, Vince took one look at my pussy and his cock stood right up to attention. He couldn't get enough of me. He was soaping me all over, all over my breasts and down my back and especially between my legs, and his hard cock was bobbing against my stomach. I took hold of his cock and stroked it for him, but he said, 'Don't . . . I'm going to shoot right here and now if you do that . . . and I want to fuck you. I just *have* to fuck you.' He opened the shower door and picked me up and carried me through to the bedroom. By that time we were both so excited that we couldn't keep our hands off each other. Vince's cock was enormous, and his balls were as tight as walnuts. He laid me down on the bed, even though we were both soaking wet, and I opened my legs as wide as I could. He ducked his head down and licked all around my pussy, and he pushed his tongue right up inside me. Then he held his cock in his fist and buried the head of his cock between my pussy lips. I reached down and spread my lips apart wider, so that I could watch his big veiny cock sliding slowly into my pussy, right up to his pubic hair. He fucked me strong and deep, but he fucked me tender, too, as if he really appreciated what I'd done for him, as if he wanted to make me feel as good as he could. He was slow and he was sweet, and sometimes he slid his cock in as far as it would go, and other times he took it half out, so that I could see my pussy lips clinging around the head of it. There's no question that hairless pussy lips are totally sexy, you can see everything and feel everything, and I could massage my lips and clitoris with my fingers while he was fucking me, which turned me on even more.

"Vince had never fucked me like this, not even at night, when he was feeling horny. Right at the end he took his cock out of me and started to jerk himself off, and I rubbed my clitoris faster and faster. I guess you could we were having a masturbating race. I came first. I tried to close my thighs together, it's your natural reaction when you have an orgasm, but Vince kept them wide apart, and then he climaxed, too, and sprayed sperm all over my pussy, big white drops of it shooting everywhere. I massaged it into my clitoris and between my lips and I took hold of his cock in my other hand and pulled Vince nearer to me. His cock was going soft, but there was a long string of sperm dangling from it, and I stuck out my tongue and let it drip right onto the middle of it, and then I swallowed it. I took the whole of his cock into my mouth and sucked it. It tasted wonderful, and because it was soft I could get all of it into my mouth at once."

Sexual teasing is one of the easiest ways to liven up your sexual relationship because it's so light-hearted, and if your partner really isn't in the mood for love, you can simply give him a kiss and try again later without him feeling that he's seriously rebuffed you or *you* feeling that you've made a fool of yourself by lighting candles and lying on the sofa in your sexiest negligée with mood music playing and a bottle of champagne on ice when all he wants to do is take a shower, open a beer, and watch the Superbowl.

If your early morning teasing succeeds and you manage to have sex before breakfast, don't think that's the end of it for the day. Keep the sexual heat simmering by *touching* him playfully; by *dressing* sexy; and by *talking* suggestively. You may have been lovers for a long time, but that's no reason for you to stop flirting with him. Be flirtatious with other men, too: that's one of the greatest teases of all. Arouse his jealousy and remind him why he was so attracted to you in the first place.

THE SECRETS OF SEXUAL PLAY

It's the little things that can bring fun back into your sex life. Cuddling up to him when he's sitting on the couch watching TV and feeling his penis through his pants. Walking into the den while he's working and massaging his shoulders for him. At bedtime, playfully undressing him—unbuttoning his shirt and pulling down his pants. Teasing your partner is a way of showing him that you find him irresistible without being all melodramatic about it, and a way of eliciting a sexual response that will probably surprise you in its intensity.

Remember that men are always looking for signals that women are sexually interested. In some ways, they are seeking permission to make a sexual advance. This has always been so, but it has been exacerbated by the laws against sexual harassment. But even in long-term relationships, a man can become cautious about approaching his partner for sex because she might well say that she's far too busy or she's just done her hair or she doesn't particularly feel like it, and that will leave him with a feeling of rejection, however nonchalantly he appears to take it. However, these days especially, women can't always expect men to make the first move, particularly if women don't make it clear that they would be very receptive if men did.

How many times have I heard a woman complain that her partner "hardly ever makes love to me," while the partner says that "when she goes to bed, she turns her back to me and that's it. How was I to know that she wanted me to make love to her?" One of the most common sexual misunderstandings of our time. *She* wanted him to show her how much he loved her by forcibly rolling her over and having his wicked way with her. He thought she simply wasn't interested in making love. Result: a serious sexual problem that could, over the months, get worse and worse, until the couple are scarcely making love at all.

That's where teasing comes in. When you tease, you make it crystal clear that you still find your partner sexy, even if you're not ready for full intercourse then and there. At times your partner may find your sexual frivolousness irritating, in which case you can simply hold off for a while. But there's no doubt that he will find it extremely flattering and a tonic for his sexual self-esteem.

"We had a dinner party for six of our friends," said Hannah, 35, a social worker from Los Angeles, California. "Among our guests was a man called Leonard, who's a movie producer. Leonard is handsome, charming, witty . . . he always has women eating out of his hand. My husband, Jake, hates having him around because of the way that Leonard can always make me sparkle. He makes every woman sparkle, it's just a talent. Actually, I think he's incredibly shallow and I couldn't even begin to think of having an affair with him. Well, maybe a one-night stand, he's very attractive, but not an affair.

"The night of our dinner party Jake was in a sulk because of Leonard. He wouldn't cheer up no matter what. I could understand it. There are times when I've felt jealous myself, and it's awful. It's like having lead in your veins and no matter what you do you can't lighten up. Halfway through the evening, when both of us were in the kitchen, I said to Jake, 'Come here,' and I kissed him. Not just a peck, a real kiss. And then I tugged down his zipper, and took his cock out of his pants, and I knelt down on the kitchen floor in my evening dress and I gave his cock a long, lascivious suck. I didn't hurry, even though we had guests waiting and there was always a chance that one of them might walk in and catch us. I made sure that his cock came up big and hard, and I took it as far into my mouth as I could, and I looked up at him with his cock bulging out of the side of my cheek. Then I zipped him up again, and kissed him again, and said, 'That's the first installment . . . more later.'

"Jake changed after that. No matter how much I flirted with Leonard, he knew that I was his, and after dinner, when we are all sitting around and talking, I made a point of sitting close to Jake and showing everybody how sexy I thought he was.

"That night, I did a striptease for him in the

bedroom, singing "The Stripper" and throwing my clothes all over the bedroom. Jake went for me and I ran away from him, jumping on the bed and dodging out of the bedroom door, flinging my bra at him as I went. He chased me downstairs and I went and hid in the broom closet . . . but not before I hung my panties on the door handle as a clue. He opened the closet and caught me, and we were both laughing like kids. Maybe it was the wine. Maybe it was more than the wine. Maybe it was the way that I'd teased him all through dinner, and made him feel that I needed him and I wanted him . . . that I was his. Maybe it was the fun of taking sex a little less seriously."

You can sexually tease your partner in so many ways. Linda, a 28-year-old ceramic artist from Cedar Rapids, Iowa, said that her sex life had been going through "kind of a dull patch." So she painted a small self-portrait of herself wearing nothing but a baseball cap and a pair of socks and packed it into her husband, John's, lunchpail. "It was *extremely* risqué," she said. "You know, legs open, like *Hustler* or something. I don't know what would have happened if any of his colleagues had seen it. I wrote a little note underneath saying, 'Vacancy needs filling . . . urgently. Must be very hard worker.'

"I didn't know how John would take it, but when he came home from work I was wearing exactly what I was wearing in the painting . . .

baseball cap and socks and nothing else. We didn't even make it to the couch. He fucked me standing up in the hallway, with my face pressed against the mirror and my bottom sticking out. He said that he'd been thinking about nothing else all day."

Men tend to go to work and absorb themselves in their working day without thinking about their partners more than a couple of times; and even then, not sexually. On the other hand, women who work at home have ample opportunity to think about sex and what they're going to do for their partner when he returns, and because of that they're much more sexually wound up at the end of the working day.

You should keep teasing your man sexually even when he's away from you, in fact, *especially* when he's away from you. Men who go away on business trips tend not to think of the partners they have left behind as lovers, but as someone who represents home and security; and you should remind your man that you're not just the keeper of the nest, his cook and cleaner, and mother of his children, but a woman with strong sexual desires which it's his job to satisfy.

In Sylvia's case, she was a career woman rather than a homemaker, and her own working day was as crowded as Peter's, but I suggested that she should still arouse his erotic interest during the day by sending him messages and pictures and items of clothing. They had to be *fun*. They had to be titillating. It was no use sending him letters saying that he was the world's most fantastic lover and that she couldn't wait to fall into his gymtoned arms again. That would simply have reinforced his sexual ideas about himself and done nothing to bring back the lighthearted sharing that their relationship had lost.

Peter had asked her the previous week why she rarely did any baking anymore, and that gave her an idea for a particularly erotic picture. Unlike Linda, she had no drawing talent, but she took a Polaroid picture of herself lying on the kitchen counter surrounded by mixing bowls and wooden spoons and flour jars. She was completely naked except for a dusting of flour over her breasts and her thighs, and she was pushing a wooden pastry pin deep into her vagina. Her caption (and it was her own idea) was: "If I'd known you were coming, I would have baked a cake."

Peter's reaction? "Stunned, I think. That's the only word I can think of. It was so different, so unexpected, so off-the-wall. He'd formed a totally fixed idea in his mind of what I was like and what our relationship was like, and that picture came completely from left field. He'd never thought of me as being somebody who was capable of being sexually outrageous. I had the feeling that he was jealous of me for having sexual thoughts outside of our relationship . . . for doing something sexual when he wasn't there, even though I'd done it to turn him on."

Had it succeeded? "Oh, yes. It turned him on all right. It made him very possessive, too. He tried to make light of it, you know? The first thing he said when he got home was, 'Where's the cake?' Then he said, 'I ought to sue that pastry pin for adultery.' But then he got more serious and he took me straight through to the bedroom and took off my clothes and made love to me. He wasn't nearly so athletic this time. He was very turned on, very rough, very aggressive. I felt like he wanted to fill me up with his cock so that I wouldn't want anything else. He didn't change position at all. He just kept pushing himself into me and saying, 'How do you like that? Is that big enough for you?' I clung onto him tight and dug my fingernails into his back and for the first time in a long time he managed to get me close to having an orgasm.

"He had a shower afterward and I finished myself off with my fingers—just one of those quiet, quiet orgasms. But I really felt that we'd made some progress."

Sylvia continued her teasing almost every day with notes, pictures, and occasional phone calls. "I called him during a meeting once and said, "This is your Oral Sex Service. If you wish to have your cock sucked when you return home from work please say 'Yes' now. If you wish to have your cock sucked and all your come swallowed, say 'Yes, Yes!' and make sure you sound like you mean it."

Peter said, "Yes, yes!" in front of all his work colleagues, and Sylvia kept her word. "As a matter of fact I was quite apprehensive. I had never swallowed any man's semen before and I was worried that I was going to choke or gag. But when it actually happened it was wonderful. His cock spurted all this slippery stuff into my mouth. I can't describe the taste. Sweet, dry, strange. It's not like anything else I ever tasted. But the next morning I felt like more of it and I sucked him out before he went to work. That was the first time I'd ever seen him reluctant to go."

One morning Sylvia tucked one of her thongs into Peter's pants pocket. "I'd worn it two days running, and I pinned a little note on it, saying 'Smell this and think of me.' Then, on the other side, I wrote, 'Make sure you're wearing this when you come home tonight. I want to see you pose for me.'

"Peter told me that as soon as he found the thong and the note he went to the men's room and changed into it. His cock was so stiff that it could hardly fit into it, and his balls bulged out on each side, but he wore it all the same. He said he could feel the elastic up between the cheeks of his ass and every time he sat down it reminded him of me.

"When he got home, I touched my finger

against his lips and I wouldn't let him speak. I undressed him until he was wearing nothing but my thong, with his cock sticking out of the side of it. I didn't take it off. I said, 'You're extremely naughty for wearing my clothes. I'm going to have to punish you. Come to the bedroom.' That was the first time Peter really started laughing. We wrestled on the bed and I climbed on top of him and sat on his cock. He didn't try to roll me over onto my back. He didn't try to take over at all. He saw how much I was enjoying myself and I guess he realized that *he* was enjoying himself, too."

Provocative Dressing is a form of sexual teasing, too; but it's obviously a little less spontaneous, particularly if you're into the full Fredericks of Hollywood regalia. You've probably seen them advertised: breast-exposing basques, peephole bras, G-strings decorated with marabou feathers, black garter belts, fishnet stockings, and stiletto heels.

Some men are really excited by classic erotic underwear like this, and even if you think that it's dated, it can still be good for a very entertaining evening. You can't really be serious when you're dressed up like a Las Vegas stripper or a Dodge City hooker, but you can have a very, very sexy kind of fun.

If you look through the small ads in women's and men's magazines, you'll find dozens of mail-order companies selling erotic underwear from silk teddies to chamois-leather thongs so if you're interested in dressing up in something fantastic you'll have plenty of choices. I carried out an informal survey of fourteen mail order companies marketing erotic underwear and on average the top ten favorites for women were:

1. lace or see-through thongs
2. garter belts and stockings
3. breast-baring negligées
4. quarter-cup bras
5. peephole bras
6. topless satin basques
7. fishnet playsuits
8. open-crotch satin panties
9. leather harnesses
10. rubber panties.

One new garment that caught my eye recently was the Butterfly, which is a very pretty white lacy panty designed to look as if a large butterfly has spread its wings across the lower part of your stomach. It has a smooth satin back, but the butterfly leaves your vulva exposed, so that you can enjoy oral sex or intercourse while you're still wearing it.

For the dominatrix in you, there's a thong made of black leather straps, buckles, and chrome-plated chains. The crotch is completely open, except for a chain that runs between the lips of your vagina and up between the cheeks of your buttocks. One of the new bestsellers, however, is a black see-through catsuit that covers your entire body from ankles to neck but leaves your breasts bare.

Rubber remains popular, and there have been record sales for black rubber women's panties with two rubber dildoes fixed in the crotch—one thick and one thinner—for all-day sexual stimulation, both vaginal and anal. A male version with a single rear dildo is also popular, as are male briefs that have a specially shaped front to contain a man's erect penis and testicles, so that the wearer can have intercourse without taking them off.

In fact, there is almost as much of a variety of erotic underwear for men as there is for women, and some of it is very playful indeed, such as G-strings with an elephant's face on the front, so that your lover's penis takes the place of the trunk. There are lace and see-through briefs for men, as well as so-called "posing pouches" in anything from black velvet to sheer pink nylon.

You don't have to be a card-carrying fetishist to get an erotic thrill out of PVC and rubber underwear, either. You can dress your man in a black high-gloss PVC jockstrap or a studded leather codpiece or transparent plastic shorts; or maybe a black PVC Edwardian bathing costume that leaves his genitals exposed. A true fetishist is somebody who can't achieve sexual gratification without a particular stimulus (such as high-heeled shoes or rubber clothing). But anybody can find fetish clothing sexually arousing, and there's absolutely nothing perverted about dressing up in leather and chains and PVC if you find it enjoyable. It can form the basis for some wild and wonderful sex play.

Laura, a 25-year-old pharmacist's assistant from Chicago, Illinois, bought several items of erotic underwear by mail order—"mostly stuff that I normally wear, like thongs and bras. They do a very attractive matching set which I've never been able to find in any store." But she was also tempted by a small pair of shiny black PVC panties. "I'm not sure why . . . maybe the model in the catalog looked a little like me, tall, big boobs, long legs, black hair. I just thought they looked very kinky and sexy so I bought them."

She guessed that her boyfriend Leo would find them exciting, but she didn't realize how much. "He works only three blocks away from me, so most days we meet for lunch. He came into the drugstore and walked right through to the store-room at the back, like he usually does. There was nobody else there but us. I told him I had to put some pills away on the top shelf and I climbed up on the stepladder. He said, 'Steady,' and put his hand on my thigh, a little way up my skirt. Then, when I came down, he slid his hand further up, and touched me between my legs. It was then that he discovered I was wearing these plastic panties.

"He couldn't believe it. He put his hand on my

butt to make sure that they were real. He said, 'What are you *wearing*?' and so I looked around to make sure that nobody else could see us, and I lifted up my skirt to show him. Black, super-shiny PVC panties, and they were so tight that you could see my pussy bulging underneath them. I mean, they really *clung*.

"Leo stroked them and ran his fingers between my legs. He said, 'Those are amazing. You've given me such a hard-on it's hurting.' I came up close to him and kissed him and said, 'I thought you might like them.' He said, '*Like* them? They're unbelievable!'

"I knew it was a risk, but I was really turned on, too. I said, 'If you behave yourself, I'll wear them in bed tonight. And if you're very, very good to me, I'll let you take them off.' I was only playing, you know, but when I was wearing those panties I could act like I was serious. 'And for now,' I said. 'You can have a little taste of them. Get down on your knees.' Leo went down on his knees and I lifted up my skirt. He kissed my bare thighs and then he kissed and licked my pussy through my panties. They were so tight that he couldn't even slip his finger inside them, but he managed to take a mouthful of my plastic-covered pussy and suck it.

"He stood up and kissed me, and I tugged open his zipper and took out his cock. It was totally rigid and it felt so big that I could hardly close my hand around it. I held him close and steered his cock until it was pressed right up against the front of my panties. Then I slid it up and down against my pussy, and it made a kind of a soft, squeaking noise—hard purple cock sliding up and down over shiny black PVC.

"I turned around and bent right over, holding on to the stepladder for support. Leo pushed his cock in between my thighs, and I reached between my legs and pressed his cock against my pussy. In fact I used his cock to masturbate myself. I pressed it harder and harder, and the squeaking grew quicker and quicker, and Leo was saying, 'Oh, I want to fuck you . . . I want to pull down your panties and fuck you . . .' That was what *I* wanted, too, but it was far too dangerous to start fucking in the storeroom . . . anybody could have walked right in at any second.

"Leo's cock was pouring out slippery juice and it was all over my fingers. I pushed him harder and harder against my pussy and I think if he could have lasted two or three minutes more, I would have come. But suddenly he grabbed my hips and he climaxed, right into my hand.

"About two seconds later, my boss walked right into the storeroom, carrying a bag with his lunch in it. I don't know how Leo managed to zip himself up so quickly without catching his cock in his zipper. He was still pretty stiff. I put my hand into the pocket of my skirt to wipe off the sperm, but

when I took it out again there was still some clinging between my fingers and I had to quickly suck
it off. Well, I didn't really have to, but I was still
turned on and I love the taste of it. And you
should have seen Leo's face.

"That night, I was still wearing the panties
when Leo came back from the office. He tried to
put his hand up my skirt so that he could feel them
again but I wouldn't let him. I said he had to take
off all of his clothes and get down on the floor and
beg me to take them off. We were both laughing
but we were playing a game, you know, and he
had to abide by the rules. So he stripped off all of
his clothes and got down on the kitchen floor and
kissed my feet.

"We went to the bedroom and I lay on the bed
and allowed him to peel off my panties inch by
inch. I was all wet and sweaty between my legs
and my pussy was still juicy from lunchtime, but I
ordered him to lick me clean before he could make
love to me, which he did. He lifted my hips and his
tongue slithered everywhere . . . right between the
cheeks of my ass, deep into my pussy, all around
my clitoris. I wasn't on cloud nine, I was on cloud
one hundred and nine.

"I was right on the very edge of an orgasm
when he stopped licking me. I was just about
to order him to carry on when he pushed his
cock right into me, and that was enough, that
immense cock forcing its way right up inside me,

that pushed me over. I had one of those orgasms that makes you feel like your whole existence is squeezed into a tiny ball."

Why did she think her clothing had such a dramatic effect? "I don't think it was the panties themselves. Like, I don't think that Leo is into shiny black PVC or rubber or anything like that, not for its own sake. But it was the fact that I wearing them—me, who usually wears itsy-bitsy little feminine lacy things. It was like I was making a sexual statement, you know? I want sex and you'd better give it to me but I'm going to make you beg for it first. It took him completely by surprise that I could be so upfront. That I could be wearing these panties without even telling him."

Laura pretty much hit the nail on the head when she talked about the surprise value of her PVC panties. As we've discussed before, surprise is one of the great aphrodisiacs, and you can use the way you dress (or undress) to give your partner a mind-blowing erotic experience just when he least expects it. Leave your panties at home when he takes you out to the movies or a barbecue or a dinner party and then tell him halfway through the evening that you're enjoying natural ventilation. It may be one of the oldest techniques in the book but it's 100 percent guaranteed to reawaken his sexual interest in you. You'll be pleasantly surprised yourself how possessive and attentive he suddenly becomes.

Again, it's a game. By playing the part of a hot-blooded, free-spirited woman, you're refocusing his attention on your sexual appetite, and showing him that he needs to be more attentive. Sylvia tried the no-panties ploy on Peter during a company cocktail party, and the result, she said "was truly startling. Peter kept his arm around me almost all evening, and he would hardly let any other man offer me a peanut, let alone flirt with me. When we got back to our apartment building, he put his hands up my dress while we were still in the elevator . . . he just couldn't wait any longer."

Try greeting your man in the evening wearing a silk blouse with most of the buttons undone . . . and no bra. Or wearing nothing but one of his shirts, with the sleeves rolled up. Or open the door in a small knitted top and a pair of sloppy socks and that's all. Or a black garter-belt and black stockings and very high heels. Or jeans and no top. Or absolutely nude, except for a beret and big hoop earrings. And play the part for which you've dressed yourself, too. Sophisticated and purring if you're going braless in a silk blouse; girlish and defenseless if you're wearing one of his shirts; hippie and cool if you're topless in jeans.

Almost always, you will find that your partner joins in your game and plays his part as if he's been rehearsing for it. After all, you've made him a surprise offer of sexual pleasure, and he won't want to spoil the fantasy.

The dressing game is so easy to play and it has such a dramatic effect on sexual relationships that have become a little humdrum that you really ought to try it. Corinne, 33, a nurse from Boise, Idaho, said that she roused her husband, Brett, by washing the car in nothing but a thin white T-shirt. "I was a one-woman wet T-shirt contest, and I won." Jeannie, a 41-year-old realtor from Napa, California, changed into a red negligée just before bedtime . . . a negligée that came with matching panties, but that left her breasts completely exposed. "All my married life, I've always dressed very demure . . . suddenly, there I was, the scarlet woman, with my breasts showing."

If you dress sexily, you don't have to say a word. You don't even have to say "I love you and I want you to make love to me tonight." Your clothes—or the lack of them—will say it all for you. You are giving your partner permission to make love to you then and there. You are encouraging him without having to give him any explanations. Even if you've dressed up to stimulate him because you don't think he gives you enough sexual attention, or you think that his lovemaking's dull, he won't see it as an implied criticism. So you'll be able to get more loving out of him without having to nag him or make him feel inadequate—neither of which are particularly good for the well-being of your sexual relationship, or for your partner's sexual performance.

The Peeping Game: Even if you've lived with your partner for a long time, don't forget that he can still be aroused by unexpected glimpses of you dressing or undressing. Men are highly responsive to visual stimuli, and you can play all kinds of games without him being aware that you're arousing him on purpose.

Rita, a 32-year-old grade school teacher from Camden, New Jersey, said that she had known for a long time that when her partner Colin was sitting up in bed reading he could see her in her full-length bathroom mirror—so long as she left the door ajar a little way. "I know he watches me when I'm undressing, and if he's watching me he must find it a turn-on, so I can't complain about that, can I? I could just as easily undress right in front of him, and quite often I do, but it's not the same, is it? If I undress right in front of him he can't really stare at me, can he? I mean he can't take a good long look, as if I were a stripper or the centerspread girl in *Playboy* magazine.

"I guess it's like putting on a show for him. I undress real slow, and I kind of smoothe my hands down my body, the way that strippers do. I take off my bra, and cup by breasts in my hands in front of the mirror, and squeeze them. Then I step out of my panties, and I always make sure that he can only see my back view first. Then at last I turn around, with my hand covering my pussy for a moment or two . . . just to prolong his frustration. But at last I lift both hands to pin up my hair, and he can see everything.

"I shave my pussy twice a week, and sometimes I do it in front of the mirror so that he can watch. I squirt a big pile of shaving foam between my legs, and then I very carefully shave away all of my hair, opening my pussy lips with my fingers so that I can get to every single one. Colin has never said a word about watching me, but I know for a fact that he does, because I've slipped my hand into his pajamas after he's seen me shaving and his cock is always swollen and juicy at the end."

You should take it as a compliment that your partner is aroused by the sight of your body and that he is sexually curious about you. I've always encouraged lovers to examine each other sexually— to show each other their bodies openly and freely. But many women are reserved about blatantly exposing themselves, and they can use the Peeping Game to satisfy their partner's desire simply to look at them.

Jayne, a 25-year-old hairdresser from Austin, Texas, said that her sexual relationship with her husband, Ken, had been "really hot" to start with, but that he had become increasingly involved with his successful driveway-surfacing business and during that period he usually came home late in the evening feeling exhausted and not in the mood for sex. "Even when business eased off, he seemed to have gotten out of the habit of making love to me. It was like we were physically strangers again. He never came into the shower with me anymore, the way he used to, and if I came into the bathroom to use the toilet he either walked out of the room or didn't look . . . and there was a time when he *always* used to look. He used to say it was the sexiest sight in the world, watching me pee.

"I felt that he was shy of me. Because we hadn't had regular sex for so long, he didn't know how to approach me anymore. I felt I had to show him that he didn't need to be shy, that he didn't have to treat me so polite all the time. It was almost like he felt that he needed to seduce me all over again, from square one. You know, candelit dinners and roses.

"One Saturday afternoon he had to go out to give somebody an estimate for a new driveway. It was a real warm day, and so I lay on a sunbed on the back verandah, which is totally private. I was thinking about sex with Ken and I was feeling pretty frustrated. I slid my hand into my shorts and started to play with myself. It was then that I heard the front door close and I realized that Ken was back. He came into the back parlor and stopped by the window when he saw me. He didn't know that I knew he was there, but I could see his reflection in the half-open door.

"I don't quite know why, but I didn't stop playing with myself. I unbuttoned my shorts all the way down, and kept on massaging my cunt with my fingers. Ken was watching me all the time, not moving, and that excited me even more. I pushed my shorts right off, and I pulled off my T-shirt, too, so that I was naked. I lay back on the sunbed and opened my legs up wide and rubbed my clitoris and slid my fingers into my cunt. I was so juicy that my cunt was making kissing noises. I worked my left middle finger into my asshole, and then my right middle finger right next to it, and stretched my asshole wide open. Of course I couldn't see Ken's face, but I could imagine it.

"I remembered something that one of my friends had done at school. She was the sexy one in the class, always flirting with boys. In fact I think it was her who taught me how to masturbate. But she did this one unbelievable thing—you had to see it. And I was so turned on, playing with myself in front of Ken, that I thought I'd try it. If *that* didn't blow his mind, then nothing would! I sat up, and turned over onto my hands and knees, so that my butt was facing toward the house. Then I reached behind me, lifted up my butt a little and slowly pushed my whole hand into my cunt, right up to the wrist. You can do it if you're juicy enough or if you use some kind of lubricant. I pushed it in and out a few times and then I turned over again and finished masturbating by rubbing my clitoris.

"I had a strange kind of orgasm, just like a whole lot of little spasms, but I guess I was kind of inhibited because I knew that Ken was watching me.

"Do you know what he did? He went back to the front door and slammed it real loud. That gave me just enough time to put on my shorts and my T-shirt. Then he came out onto the verandah like he'd just arrived home. He acted all casual and nonchalant, but he gave me an incredible kiss, and he was all round me for the rest of the day, hugging me and kissing me. He opened a bottle of wine and then he said, 'Do you know something, I think I've been working too hard. I think I've been neglecting you. What say we have a really early night tonight? Like *now*?'

"As far as I'm concerned, if you can find a way to show your man that you're a sexy person who's longing for some good loving, you'll be doing yourself a very great favor."

Sylvia tried something similar by pretending to be asleep one evening when Peter came back from work late . . . lying on the bed with her pink nightshirt up around her waist and her legs a little way apart. Peter came in and sat beside her and stroked her hair but she kept up the pretense that she was asleep, which gave him the opportunity to look at her sexually for as long as he wanted, without feeling embarrassed about it. As I have said many times before, men are aroused simply by looking, and if your partner finds it erotically stimulating to look at *you*, then you should be proud and pleased.

Peter left her to "sleep" and then came in later to wake her. "Something had changed between us. It's hard to pin down exactly what it was. But I think we had both remembered why we were attracted to each other in the first place. We remembered that we loved to touch each other, to kiss each other, to sit in each other's arms. We remembered the fun and the laughter."

Flirting and teasing and a little bit of erotic dressing-up could bring back more fun and laughter into your sexual relationship than you can imagine, or enhance the fun and the laughter that you already have. But let's take it further. Let's see how you can use sexual play to bring drama and sparkle into your relationship, and at the same time use it to improve some of those aspects of your lovemaking about which you may not be altogether confident.

•

6
A Role in the Hay

We all lack self-confidence, even the brashest of us. I have talked to some very well-known actors and TV personalities, and it is always a surprise to discover how nervous they are before they appear in public. As one TV interviewer said, "I'm just as scared as everybody else, but the reason I'm good at my job is because I've learned not to show it."

Almost all of us find it easier to put on something of an act in our social lives. We invent a personality that we would like other people to think we are, and we play out that role in order to mask our own lack of self-confidence. We try to present ourselves in a way that will impress other people, and we do everything we can to conceal our weaknesses and our oddities and our uncertainties.

How many times have you come across a man who—when you first meet him—appears to be smooth and confident and totally in control, but who soon turns out to be a mess of unresolved psycho-sexual problems, with a life that is about as organized as a Marx Brothers movie? He was acting, he was playing a part. And don't try to pretend that you haven't done the same—trying to come on like a sophisticated woman of the world whose last lover had his own private plane, instead of a librarian with a Band-Aid holding your glasses together.

But you can play parts in your life without deceiving people, provided they're aware of what you're doing, and provided they're happy to join in, and this is particularly rewarding when it comes to sex. Playing sexual games can help you understand your own sexual personality and your partner's sexual personality, too. It can help you to answer any questions you may have about your sexual relationship, such as, should I really be having an affair with this man? Do we really hit it off together in bed? Am I satisfied? Is he? Or are we both concealing something from each other? Is our relationship going to blossom into something more, or is it all raw sex and nothing else?

Sexual play can tell you if your long-term partner is harboring any unfulfilled sexual fantasies about you, and whether or not you would be wise to let him try them out. It can also help you to try out *your* sexual fantasies, in a way that your partner will find not only acceptable but highly arousing.

Sexual play can also help you to improve your sexual technique, by giving you the courage to try things that you may not have tried before, or by giving you the opportunity to indulge yourself much more fully in those things that you may have tried, but are still not really confident about. For instance, oral sex. The single most frequently expressed anxiety that I receive in my mail is *How do I know if I'm any good at oral sex?* Then I get all kinds of questions, like *I never get aroused until my boyfriend has almost finished;* or simply *I don't know how to respond during sex . . . should I talk, should I cry out, should I jump around, or should I stay still? My last boyfriend loved me talking dirty in his ear. My new boyfriend says it distracts him and tells me to shut up.*

It isn't difficult to introduce sexual play into your love life. For instance, let's suppose that you have a reasonably stable relationship with the man in your life, but you're not at all sure that you're giving him the satisfaction he really expects. And why aren't you sure? Because he's not really giving you the satisfaction that *you* expect. You feel that there's something missing in the dynamics of your sex life.

Don't try to meet a sexual problem like this head-on. You may feel that you can say absolutely anything to your partner. But it is certainly not a positive course of action to say, "Look . . . something's wrong with our sex life. I don't feel satisfied when you make love to me, and I don't think I'm satisfying you, either."

If you take that approach, you might just as well say *sayonara* there and then. Lack of sexual satisfaction is almost impossible to quantify. So you don't think you're having enough orgasms? That's reasonably easy to put right. But what if you don't think you're getting enough excitement, or enough passion? Talking can never solve a problem like that, no matter how full and frank you are. If your partner wasn't already aware that something wasn't quite clicking, you'll only succeed in making him feel bewildered and inadequate. If he *has* been conscious of it, you'll only succeed in making him feel even more frustrated and depressed than he is already.

To build or repair a really good sex life, you need to be optimistic, lighthearted, and *positive*. You may lack confidence in yourself, but then we *all* do, and one of the most effective ways of overcoming a lack of confidence is to play a part—to *act* the role of the kind of lover you'd like to be, and to encourage your partner to act the role of the kind of lover you'd like *him* to be.

Conjure up in your mind the sex life you really want. Do you want it to be more passionate, more romantic, more exciting, more extreme? Do you want to be carried up the stairs like Scarlett

O'Hara or do you want to taken up against a wall like the woman in *9½ Weeks*? Do you want dominant or submissive? Exhibitionistic or coy? Do you want longer and more creative foreplay? Or do you simply want more of the sex that you're getting already?

Use your imagination in the same way you did when you were playing games as a young girl. Don't be embarrassed by your own fantasies. Bring them out of the closet like the dress-up clothes you used to put on. You're going to use them to remodel your love life and bring you all the excitement that your sexual relationship has been lacking.

So how do you initiate a sexual game? Here are five practical examples of women who wanted to spice up their love lives and succeeded—not only by playing a part but by encouraging their partners to play a part, too.

Barbara is a 26-year-old legal secretary from San Francisco, California. She had been living for two and a half years with Chris, 30, an architect who was introduced to her by one of her best friends. To begin with, Barbara felt that she and Chris were an ideal couple in every way, but as time went by she began to discover that Chris became less affirmative than he used to be, and that he was depending on her more and more to make domestic decisions—what they should eat or where they should eat, what TV program they should watch, what time they should go to bed ... and even if they should make love or not.

"After a while I felt that I was running the whole relationship," said Barbara. "I think the problem was that I'm a very organized person, and the more I organized everything, the less responsibility Chris took for what was going on. He could be extremely masterful, but like most men I think he wasn't basically interested in the day-to-day running of his life—even his sex life—and provided everything was going smoothly he was quite happy to leave everything to me."

I asked Barbara what her ideal sex life would be. Without any hesitation, she said, "I always wanted to be cosseted, treated like somebody's little girl, I always wanted a man who would take care of me and look after me and show me the best time in bed." Which was just about the polar opposite of what Chris was giving her. "He was good in bed, when he made an effort, but he was usually satisfied with straightforward sexual intercourse and he never bothered too much with foreplay. So of course the consequence was that I was often left feeling frustrated; and I don't think he found our lovemaking very satisfying, either. He got his rocks off, if you'll excuse the expression, but that's about as far as it went. I'm sure he was aware that our sex life could have been better, but I don't think he had any idea how to go about improving it—and I don't think he had the incentive, either.

"I was initiating most of our lovemaking, so all he had to do was fuck me and fall asleep."

I suggested to Barbara that she play the "little girl" part that she had always fantasized about. Like many organized and organizing people, she had allowed herself to take over too much control of her relationship with Chris—the housework, the accounts, the daily routine—to the point where he didn't even have to think when to make love to her. Organizing people find it difficult to delegate, and even harder to let things slide, but that's what Barbara had to do if she were going to become the sexually cosseted nymphet of her dreams, and if Chris was going to start becoming masterful on a full-time basis.

"Usually I get out of bed first and make an early morning cup of coffee, but that Wednesday morning I stayed where I was. About a quarter of eight Chris suddenly lifted his head from the pillow and said, 'What time is it? I have to get to work! How about that coffee?' But all I did was snuggle up to him and put my arm around him and start to play with his cock. I said. 'You can be late today, can't you?' He said, 'No, I can't! I have this real important meeting.' But I wouldn't let him go. I kept pulling at his cock and even though he knew that he had to get out of bed, he stayed where he was. His cock grew harder and harder until it was sticking up like a dog's bone. He rolled over and tried to climb on top of me, but I kept my thighs tight together so that he couldn't get his cock into me. He was quite angry. He said, 'What are you doing? First you get me all horny and then you won't let me do it! What gives?'

"I acted all girly with him. I said, 'How do I know that you really love me?' He said, 'I wouldn't be here, would I, if I didn't.' But I said, 'If you loved me, you'd kiss me.' But at the same time I kept on stroking and tickling his cock and his balls. He kissed me and then he said, 'There! Satisfied?' But I said, 'No. If you loved me, you'd kiss me like you wanted to eat me.' So he kissed me, and this time it was a long, lingering kiss, and then it was tongues; and then we started to kiss the way we used to kiss, when we first fell in love with each other. Isn't it incredible how you stop doing that, after you've been living with somebody for quite a while?

"That was gorgeous, and it really turned me on, too. But when Chris tried for a second time to push his cock into me, I still kept my thighs together and I twisted my hips sideways so that he couldn't. He said, 'Come on, now, Barbara, what are you trying to do to me here?'

"I said, 'If you *really* loved me, you'd kiss my breasts, too.' So that's what he did, he kissed my breasts and sucked my nipples and he really relished it. It was exciting, to have all that attention lavished on my breasts, but I deliberately play-acted that he was stimulating my breasts so much that I was practically having an orgasm. It's surprising, though, isn't it? When you start play-acting at being turned on, with all that gasping and panting and lifting your hips, it does actually turn you on, you can feel it.

"Chris seemed to forget about putting his cock into me in such a hurry. He kept on kissing and squeezing and massaging my breasts, and gently tugging my nipples with his teeth. Then he knelt over me, and rubbed the head of his cock against my nipples and around my breasts. He opened the hole in his cock with his finger so that my nipples could poke into it, and they were certainly stiff enough!

"He licked me, all the way down my stomach and around my hips. I have these really sensitive nerves there, and it was almost like having an electric shock. Then he started licking between my legs, even though they were tightly clenched together. He poked his tongue in between my thighs and slowly slid it upward. As it approached my cunt I felt like opening my legs up wide, but I didn't, I kept them tightly closed, even when he started licking around my mound of Venus, trying to force his tongue down into my cunt.

"He was desperate for it. He was actually desperate to give me foreplay. And all the time I was putting on this act of being a prick-teasing little girl—gasping and moaning whenever he licked me or kissed me or ran his fingers down my sides,

173

but keeping my legs closed so that he couldn't fuck me.

"At last he began to realize that I was playing some kind of a game and that if he wanted to make love to me he would have to start playing it, too. He came up and kissed me again, and then he said, 'I've got you now,' and he was actually laughing. He turned around in bed and went right down to my feet. He took my right foot in his hand and licked all around my toes, and sucked them, too, which is really incredibly sexy, even if you're not into feet. But then he licked the sole of my foot, and went on licking it, and that is *so* tickly that I screamed with laughter and I actually peed myself a little bit.

"I said, 'Stop, stop, I've wet myself,' but he said, 'I always knew you were a naughty little girl. I'm going to have to punish you.' He opened my thighs up wide and he licked me right between my legs. His tongue was playing everywhere, all around my clitoris, between my lips, and deep into my cunthole. He even poked the tip of it into my peehole.

"Because he was turned around, his cock was right in front of me, and I took hold of it and licked it, all the way down the shaft, and around his balls. Then I took it into my mouth and sucked it hard. He flinched, and said, 'Gentle, gentle . . .' but I said in this really spoilt girlish voice, 'This is *my* sucker and I'm going to suck it as hard as I want.'

"He kept on licking me faster and faster and I heard myself gasping and this time I wasn't play-acting. That was the first time he had ever licked me to orgasm, and I couldn't believe the sensation of his tongue flickering between my legs. I grew tenser and tenser until I was clawing the sheet and I was sinking my teeth into Chris's cock. It seemed to take hours and hours before I actually came, the feeling kept rising up and rising up and I never seemed to be able to get there. But then Chris forced his cock deeper into my throat, and actually started to fuck my mouth, and I felt like I was having a fit. I blacked out for a second, and I let out another squirt of pee, which made me feel terribly hot and embarrassed, but Chris didn't mind at all, even though it went all over his face.

"He turned around and pushed his cock into my cunt, and I kept having these tiny little after-shocks. I felt so good, I stretched myself out and I opened my legs and let him fuck me slow and easy, sliding in and out, and I reached my hands down and fondled his balls and my own cunt and I let him feel that I was opening myself wide for him, that I was his, and that he could do whatever he liked with me.

"He started to fuck me faster, and I reached around and dug my fingernails into the cheeks of his ass, pulling him closer and deeper. He shouted out when he climaxed, which is something he'd never done before; and when it was over he rolled onto the bed next to me and held me close, which is something he hadn't done for a very long time, his soft wet cock lying against my thigh.

"I began to play that 'little-girly' game more often—not just in bed, but with everything. I stopped organizing our finances and I asked him to decide what he wanted for dinner and I literally forced myself to be less overpoweringly efficient around the house.

"Men like to help. They like to organize. They like to decide. But if you start to do it all for them, they quickly get to depend on you. It's the same with sex. If you're always doing the running, they'll think that when you *don't* make a move on them, you don't want it, so they won't bother."

If your man has become sexually lazy, my advice is to be more like Marilyn Monroe—a bit more breathless and ditsy. It's only an act: it doesn't mean that you're compromising your feminine equality. But men absolutely adore it. It brings out their protective instincts, and you'll find that they do a whole lot more for you than they ever did before, and that includes more lovemaking.

Notice how Barbara cleverly teased Chris into giving her more foreplay. She didn't make him feel that he wasn't very good at it. In fact she did the opposite, by exaggerating her ecstasy with moans and gasps. Although she appeared to be-having in a "little-girly" way, she was completely in charge of what was happening—even though

Chris came out of it feeling deeply satisfied and even more virile than ever.

Some men, however, respond to more obvious sexual control. These are often men who have been dominated in their early life by a strong female presence—their mother or their sisters or both. They find it difficult to be dominant in bed because they have been conditioned always to seek female approval for what they do. They're the kind of men who *ask* if they can hold your hand.

Behaving like a little girl doesn't work too well with men like these because they tend to give up at the first indication of sexual discouragement. They can be the sweetest, most considerate partners of all, but that doesn't necessarily help when you're looking for more exciting sex. There are ways, however, of bringing out the tiger in them.

Melissa, 27, works for a poodle parlor in Los Angeles, California. She met her partner Steve, a 32-year-old accountant, through his mother, who regularly brought her dogs in for trimming and clipping.

"When I first saw Steve, I couldn't believe my eyes. He is so good looking, you don't have any idea. Think of William Baldwin and you've got it. Slim, dark hair, piercing blue eyes. His mother introduced us and suggested that Steve take me out of dinner. His *mother* suggested it, can you believe it? He said, 'Sure,' as if it was the most natural thing in the world for his mother to make his social arrangements for him.

"We had dinner together and I have to say that I fell for him. He's charming, educated, funny. And his *manners*! He brought me a corsage for the evening. He opened the car door for me. He always walked on the outside of the sidewalk— you know, just in case I got splashed by mud from passing cars. He pulled out my chair for me at the restaurant. He did it all.

"The only trouble was, he couldn't make a single decision without asking me first. Should we have a cocktail before dinner? Should we have red or white wine? Should we have two courses or three?

"He's an accountant, okay, but his job's pretty interesting, because he helps to arrange finances for independent TV producers. So he wasn't boring, not at all. He'd met most of the cast of *Friends* and *ER*, too. But in spite of the fact that he was interesting and handsome, he couldn't make any personal decisions without asking for my approval, and even on that first evening together I began to think, *What is this? Can I possibly stand to have a relationship with this man?* But he was so cute that I decided to persevere.

"We went back to my place and I asked him up for coffee. I played some moody music and we sat on the couch together and he put his arm around me. I thought, *At last he's made a move without ask-*

ing first.' But do you know? About two seconds later, he said, 'I hope this is all right, my putting my arm around you?' Aggh!

"He asked me if he could kiss me. I was very patient with him and said yes. And let me tell you, he kisses like an angel. I should have been asking *him*. We had a *very* hot session on the couch, and if he had been more insistent I would have gone the whole way with him, but I didn't make a habit of going to bed with guys on the very first date, and I had the feeling that Steve needed to go home and check things out with his mother . . . like, would she approve if he took me out again, and got a little more serious?

"Maybe I was being unkind, thinking that, but it didn't really matter because he called me the next day and said that he wanted to see me again, *if I thought that was okay.* I said sure, but at the same time I made myself a promise that I was going to make a man out of him, you know?

"We went to bed together on that second date. I knew how much he wanted me but I practically had to seduce *him*. It was only when I took off his necktie and started to unbutton his shirt that I think he felt confident enough to put his hand on my breast. I'll tell you what, though, he was good at taking off my bra, which most of my boyfriends never were, and he slid off my pantyhose and my panties without getting them all rolled up together like most guys do.

"He's a good lover but very conventional. He kisses beautifully, and his fingers still give me tiny electric shocks. He's slim, almost boyish, but his cock's very big, and when he's really hard it has this upward curve, like a rhino horn. He always fucks me slowly and gently, and if he climaxes before I do, he always makes sure that he gives me an orgasm. He's just as considerate in bed as he is in a restaurant.

"Maybe you could say that I'm being ungrateful, but his lovemaking is always the same, and he always asks me if I'm ready to take his cock inside me—as if he couldn't feel for himself, with his fingers—and right in the middle of fucking he always asks me if I'm comfortable. Comfortable? Who cares about comfortable? I can remember one of my boyfriends fucking me up the ass over the hood of his Chevy Caprice, with transmission fluid for a lubricant.

"I love Steve, but I really need more out of my sex life. I need a man who's going to *take* me. A man who's going to make me feel defenseless and feminine and *used*. I need to have my panties ripped off and a good hard fuck up against a tree.

"I thought of acting all whorish, and I dressed up in red stockings and a red garter belt and G-string when I came to bed. I turned him on, but he wasn't any less polite. He even asked me if he could pull my G-string to one side so that he could put his cock in me, or would I rather take it right off? As I say, I love him, but he has to start acting like a real man, because I can't live like this for the rest of my life."

I know hundreds of women who would give a briefcase full of new hundred-dollar bills for a lover like Steve, patient, courteous, and considerate. But you can understand why Melissa felt frustrated. She's a hotblooded girl who loves exciting sex, and she could see no way of coaxing Steve into giving her the more unrestrained kind of action that she was used to.

He was obviously a skillful lover, even if his lovemaking was repetitious, and it was likely that he *knew* about most of the basic sexual variations. But it sounded to me as if he were afraid to try any sexual variations with her in case she reacted with annoyance or disgust.

She said, "I can't tell him outright that his lovemaking just isn't enough to keep me happy. I can't. I can just imagine his face if I did. He'd be shattered. I'd be lucky if he ever got another hard-on again."

Instead, I suggested that Melissa play a game with him—a game in which she was a totally domineering woman with pulled-back hair and heavy-rimmed glasses and a severe black suit, underneath which she wore a black lacy bra, black lace-topped self-support stockings, and nothing else. Oh—except for a pair of black high heels.

During his childhood years, Steve's mother had

conditioned him not only to be faultlessly polite to women, but not to do anything without their consent and approval. This was partly because he was her only child and she wanted him to grow up "perfect"—unlike his father, from whom she was divorced on the grounds of cruelty. She was an ardent feminist, who believed that women should be entitled to set the agenda in any physical relationship according to her own likes and dislikes (after all, women are the ones who are being penetrated). But she was also extremely jealous of any woman who inveigled her precious son into bed and threatened to take him away from her.

It was no good for Melissa to try acting like a vamp or a full-blown seductress or a little-girly nymphet like Barbara. Steve would continue to behave as courteously with them as he did with her normal persona. Instead, she had to act like a mother-substitute, a woman who was going to tell him exactly what to do and how to do it. She had to wrench him out of his mother's control and show him how to be unreservedly wild in bed.

"I looked terrific when I dressed up, if I say so, myself. I actually had my hair cut short and slicked back with gel. I wore a black beret and thick black glasses. I wore a suit that he had never seen before—it had wide shoulders and wide lapels and was fastened with a single button at the waist. My breasts aren't very big so I didn't bother with a bra, but I did wear the lace-topped stockings. I gelled my pubic hair, too. And you should have seen my shoes: black fetish shoes with six-inch stiletto heels.

"When Steve came back from work that night he was in the mood to celebrate. He had finished working out a deal for a new TV series and he had been given a bottle of champagne. He took one look at me and said, 'Why are you dressed like that, all in black? Has somebody died?' I went up to him and peered right into his face and said, in this jokey foreign accent, 'You have done well to-day, have you? Then I think you had better *share* your good luck, don't you?'

"He shook his head because he couldn't really understand what kind of game I was playing. He said, 'What's with the accent?' and 'What have you done to your *hair*?' I said, 'I'm going to make sure that you share your good luck, that's all.'

"He said, 'Hey—I'll pour you a glass of champagne, if you like. It's still pretty cold.' I said, 'Very good. But first of all you must take off all of your clothes.' He couldn't believe what he was hearing . . . and I can tell you that if I hadn't been play-acting, I could never have told him to undress, not outright. He hesitated for a moment, but I went right up to him and gave him a kiss, and at the same time I took his hand and slipped it inside my coat, over my breast. I said, 'Take off all of your clothes. That's an order.' He laughed and said 'Who are you kidding?' But he made the mistake of kissing me again and slipping his tongue into my mouth. I gripped it between my teeth so that he couldn't get free. I bit harder and harder until I could taste blood and in the end he managed to nod his head and say 'Okay! Okay!'

"He stripped off. He started to fold his clothes, but I told him to throw them across the room. His cock wasn't fully erect but it was very big, and his foreskin had peeled back so that the head of it was exposed. He opened the champagne and poured out two glasses. I said, 'I want to taste it first.' I took my glass and dipped his cock into it. Then I bent over and gave his cock a good sharp suck. It stiffened up even more. I said, 'Okay . . . that'll do. You can put these on.' I handed him a pair of my black see-through nylon panties, with a lace frill. He said, 'Wait a minute . . .' but I interrupted him and said, 'This evening you will do what I tell you to do. Otherwise you will be punished.'

"He put on my panties. His cock grew bigger still, and I could see it all red and stiff through the shiny black nylon. He was grinning, because he still wasn't sure that I was serious. I think he was frightened, too, but he was very turned-on and that was the most important thing. I told him to follow me through to the bedroom and, to bring the champagne.

"I said, 'Take off my coat,' which he did. Then I sat on the bed and said, 'Suck my breasts. Take my nipples right into your mouth.' He sat beside me and started to kiss my breasts, little butterfly kisses. I grabbed hold of his cock through his panties and dug my fingernails into it. I said, '*Suck*, that's what I told you to do! Suck so much breast into your mouth that it chokes you!'

"Obviously, this was like nothing he had ever done before. He sucked my breasts hard and bit at my nipples and he could tell that he was hurting me because I was gritting my teeth. But it was one of those good pains that make you feel like you're discovering something dangerous and sexy about yourself. You know—something right at the limits of what you're prepared to do.

"Then I said, 'Take off my skirt,' and he did that, too, and now he was really getting into it. I said, 'Lick my cunt, you dirty bastard. Stick your face in it,' but he didn't need much encouragement. He knelt at the end of the bed and lifted my legs over his shoulders and plunged his mouth right into my open cunt. I pulled my cunt lips wide open so that he could lick me everywhere, and it was sensational. After a couple of minutes he tried to climb up on the bed to fuck me, but I said, 'No! Keep on licking, you filthy creature! That's all you're good for!' He lifted my hips with his hands and started to lick my asshole. I looked down while he was doing it and he looked back at me. He rolled his tongue into a point and stuck it right into my asshole, and all the time we had total eye contact. It was very erotic.

"Then I beckoned him and said, 'Come here. Fuck me.' He climbed up and I pulled his cock out of his panties, just his cock. I guided it down between my legs and then I said, 'Fuck me. And I mean fuck me.' He pushed his cock into me, as deep as it would go, and it felt so good I almost purred. But he was still using that same slow rhythm that he always used. I took hold of his balls and clawed them, right through his panties, and used them to pull him toward me. I said, 'Fuck me! Don't hold out on me! Fuck me *hard*!'

"He pushed faster, and deeper, but I still kept on ordering him to fuck me harder. I dug my fingernails into his back and scratched him all the way down to his ass. Then I lifted my head up and bit his nipples, as hard as he'd been biting me, and even when he was moving up and down on me like a mad beast, I clung on to him with my teeth, until he actually shouted out 'Aaaah!' because it was hurting him.

"He was fucking me so hard now that I was sure he was going to climax at any second. I took him out of me, and turned around, and pushed his cock back into his panties. Then I masturbated him through the nylon. It only took a few seconds before he came, and I could see the sperm flooding out of his cock and spreading across the inside of his panties. He fell back on the bed, panting, and he must have thought it was all over, because he

said, 'That was outstanding. That was like nothing
I ever experienced before, ever.'

"But I said, 'Take off those panties, they're mine.
Come on, take them off, quick!' He took them off,
and I knelt on the bed on my hands and knees and
said, 'Right . . . now push them up my asshole.
Just leave an inch so that you can pull them out
again.' And he didn't complain, he did it. He
poked those wet spermy panties into my asshole,
all the way up. I said, 'You're so obedient, aren't
you, you dirty sex-mad dog. Now lick me again.
Lick me till I'm satisfied.'

"He laid his head on the pillow and I sat over
his face. His tongue really flew, it was better than
any vibrator. My cunt hole was so wet that he had
to keep swallowing. It took a long time for me to
feel my orgasm coming. Maybe I was tense about
it. In any case, I always find it more difficult when
I'm sitting up like that. But he kept on licking me
and licking me for over ten minutes and at last I
could feel myself tightening up. I took hold of his
hand and guided it around behind me so that he
was holding the end of my panties, and I said,
'When I tell you . . . when I tell you, pull them out.
Not too fast. Not too slow. As smooth as you can.'

"I started to come, and he slowed his licking
right down so that his tongue was rolling over my
clitoris all wet and warm. He pulled my panties
out of my ass, twisting them around a little as he
did so, and that made me tingle so much that I

187

could hardly stand it. And then I came, and I came, and I closed my eyes and I felt that I couldn't stop coming.

"Ever since that night, our sexual relationship has been completely different. Steve knows now that I like to try different things, and that I won't be upset or embarrassed if he dives down the bed and starts to lick my cunt, or if he pushes his finger up my asshole, or if he wants to use dirty language to turn me on. He doesn't say 'Would you like to go to bed?' anymore, he just takes me.

"I haven't changed him. Not fundamentally, I mean. He's still the politest man on the planet, and I appreciate him for that. But when it comes to sex, he's so much more confident than he used to be. I was able to show him that I get a kick out of being a little wild sometimes, and that I like to try out different things in bed. And now that he knows what I'm like, he feels free to let himself go. Only last weekend he brought us breakfast in bed, cereal and fruit. He peeled a banana, pulled back the bedcovers, and pushed it into my cunt. Then he lay between my legs and ate it—with lots of licking all around it. And a couple of times I've woken up in the middle of the night to find that he's actually fucking me, which I adore. He never would have done that before. He would have woken me up first and asked me if it was all right."

The psychology of Melissa's sexual game with Steve may have been nothing more than instinctive, but it was right on. By dressing up severely and adopting a very domineering attitude, she overrode his mother's influence on him and virtually gave him permission to take the sexual initiative whenever he felt like it. She freed him from his childhood conditioning—at least as far as sex was concerned—and showed him that women not only *expect* their lovers to be creative and positive, they *demand* it.

Her use of language was very adroit, too. When you're playing the part of a dominatrix, it's easy to make the mistake of belittling your partner and mocking his sexual prowess. This doesn't matter if he's quite confident about his virility and his sexual skills, then, it can add to his erotic pleasure, because he knows he can prove you wrong (and that's probably the reason you're doing it to begin with). But if he has any doubts about his potency or his ability to give you a good time in bed, you should avoid saying anything that makes him feel inadequate, even as a joke. It could backfire on you quite badly. Melissa didn't do this. In fact, she tried to give Steve the impression that—*aha!*—she had seen through his polite, Clark Kent–ish exterior to the horny sex god that he really was.

What surprised Melissa more than anything else, however, was how much extra confidence she had managed to conjure up when she was playing the part of a sexually domineering woman. "I didn't know I had it in me," she said. "I could hear myself ordering Steve to take off his clothes and I knew it was me but somehow I couldn't believe that it was me. Normally, I wouldn't have *dared*. But when I was play-acting, I didn't care. If Steve got mad he wouldn't be getting mad at me—not me, personally, only the character I was playing."

Steve obviously realized that, too, because it didn't take much more encouragement than a bitten tongue for him to join in with Melissa's little drama, and to play the part of the obedient stud with increasing enthusiasm.

Some people have to have few drinks before they feel confident enough to say what's on their minds. Play-acting can give you the same release from sexual inhibition without affecting your sexual prowess.

When I talk to couples these days about their sexual relationships, I keep hearing that old-fashioned word "romance" cropping up, time after time. Romance seems to have been forgotten by all of those daytime TV shows and those sophisticated women's magazines. Yet people still feel the need for romance in their sexual relationships, both men and women, even if the cynics think it's corny.

By romance, I'm not just talking about a dozen red roses or a candlelit dinner for two or a second honeymoon in Maui. I'm talking about all of those little gestures that show your partner that you care for him constantly (and that he cares for you). I'm talking about creating an atmosphere of devotion between you, because devotion can form the basis of a sexual relationship that isn't just enduring, but that can reach extraordinary heights of sensation.

The demands of modern life positively discourage romance. For instance, if you and your partner are both working, your time together will be very limited, and it isn't easy to develop a romantic ambience if you're tired and hungry and your mind is still buzzing with the problems of your working day.

That was one of the factors that contributed to Sylvia and Peter's losing focus in their sexual relationship: When they came home at night they didn't have the energy to romance each other. Instead, they were both looking for a stiff drink, a sympathetic and uncritical ear, a hot dinner, and a good night's sleep.

Working couples tend to be competitive rather than cooperative: "My work is much more demanding than yours." And this competition can quickly lead to irritable squabbles about who's more tired than whom, who's going to cook dinner, who's going to tidy the apartment, and so on. While these squabbles may not be terminal, they do have a very cooling effect on your relationship between the sheets—quite apart from the fact that you really *are* tired, and the last thing you feel like is two hours of wildly orgasmic sex.

Greater personal mobility and greater freedom for women in the workplace has also led to an increase in what used to be called "whirlwind romances." But despite the fact that they're called "romances" they can very rapidly fall victim to a lack of romance. Too often, a couple who caught each other's eye and jumped into bed together within two hours of first meeting will quickly discover that—even though they may be willing— they can only spend a certain amount of time having sex. They scarcely know each other, and so their relationship doesn't yet have a vocabulary: a favorite restaurant, a favorite song, walks by the seashore, stolen kisses, pet names. But if their sexual relationship is going to continue, and if it's going to develop from naked lust into naked lust plus deep affection, or even naked lust plus love, they're going to have to work on building up a romantic background to give their affair some depth. Without that depth, their sexual liaison will begin to mean less and less, and it will inevitably diminish into what Verlaine rather cynically described as "the meaningless friction of two glands."

Sex in marriages and long-term relationships can also be affected when you grow accustomed to each other and romance begins to fade. It's not easy to surprise somebody with whom you've been living for ten years or more, or think of some novel way of showing them how much you love them and how sexually attractive they are. Many couples forget even to say "I love you" now and again, or write each other small appreciative notes, or buy each other flowers or other small gifts. But these are all part of romance, and romance is all part of a really great sex life.

Sexual play is a wonderful way to bring romance back into your relationships. Think of all the romantic characters you'd like to be: Pocahontas or Scarlett O'Hara or Catherine the Great. Or maybe it's somebody in a movie: Ingrid Bergman or Mia Farrow or Kate Winslet. Or maybe you have imaginary romantic characters of your own.

It takes thought and planning to create a romantic atmosphere, but it will almost always pay off. You can do it with the smallest thing: by buying yourself a filmy new nightdress, or by producing a chilled bottle of champagne at bedtime (or better still, at breakfast). You can write a romantic note and leave it in your partner's pocket or wallet so that he'll discover it later. You can express sentiments in a note that sound impossibly mushy if you try to say them face to face. *"We've been together for 1,999 days today . . . and I love you more with each passing minute . . . the way you look, the sound of your voice, your touch . . . you still excite me, you still arouse me, and whenever you're not with me, I find myself wanting you so much that it's almost an ache. . . ."*

You can send your partner romantic E-mails at work, or small gifts, even if they're no more consequential than a box of his favorite candy. Don't save it for birthdays or Valentine's Day, do it because it's Thursday or because you just happen to feel like it. You don't have to do it every day, or even every week, but the more frequently you do it, the more romantically inclined he'll be, and the more inclined to send flowers and gifts and romantic notes in return.

As we've seen before, you need to surprise your partner to arouse him. Confront him with the unexpected. Again, it can be something quite small, like taking his hand and pressing it against the side of your skirt so that he comes aware that you're wearing a garter-belt and stockings. Or it can be a key in an envelope . . . a key to a motel room close to his place of work, where you'll be waiting for him in the sexiest outfit you can think of.

It *can* be the famous candlelit *diner-à-deux* but I always think that these tend to be rather strained. You've spent all afternoon cooking, and even if your partner isn't particularly hungry he's going to feel constrained to eat it, and also to tell you how delicious it is, even if he hates it. You're tense and busy and flustered. He's weighed down by the obligation to enjoy himself and also to be seductive afterward, even if he feels like doing nothing but crashing out on the couch in front of the television.

This is how Helen, a 32-year-old gift shop owner from Bangor, Maine, brought a night of romance into her relationship with Bruce, 37, an engineer. "I was married when I was twenty-two, which was far too young—well, it was for me. I was always a romantic and I was starry-eyed about the *idea* of being Mrs. John Hudson II. I had everything I wanted—the big white wedding, the honeymoon in the Caribbean. It was only when we came back from the honeymoon and had to start the business of boring old day-to-day living together that I began to realize that I had made a serious mistake.

"I was fond of John, don't get me wrong. But fond was about as far as it went. And I don't think he really loved me, either. He had fancied the idea of being married to the prettiest girl in the neighborhood, so that he could legally have sex with her every night, and then I think he had just been swept along by the whole wedding bandwagon— too scared to say 'whoa!'

"John was about the least romantic guy I ever met, and I've met some, believe me. He came home every evening, opened a beer, and sat in front of the television chewing peanuts with his mouth open. I was too young and inexperienced to change him. I thought that a wife had to do what her husband told her to do (can you imagine

195

it!) and so I never said a word. Every day was the same boring routine. We hardly even spoke to each other most evenings. John knew nothing about anything and didn't want to know, either. As far as he was concerned, life was getting up, going to work, coming back, eating dinner, watching television until you felt tired, and then going to bed. Oh, and fucking your wife two or three times a week. Not romancing her, not making her feel as if she were the sexiest woman on earth. Just getting on top of her and making the bed squeak. If you asked me what was the most interesting thing about making love to John I would have to say that it was looking at the crack on the bedroom ceiling.

"We were divorced after three and a half years. After that I didn't have another sexual relationship for eighteen months. Then I met Frater. He was the most unreliable man *ever*, and I could never believe a word he said, but he was a high-powered romantic. The day after he met me he came into the china and glass store where I worked, carrying a bunch of lilies so huge that it was totally ridiculous, and he vaulted over the counter to give them to me. He had a white Dodge Charger and he used to take me for rides in it, right up into the woods, and then he would take me into a clearing and spread out a blanket and open up a bottle of wine. We made love naked in the woods, and Frater was absolutely insatiable.

He used to fuck me, and then he would lie back and look at the sky, but it wasn't long before he started getting restless again, and kissing me, and then going down on me and kissing my pussy.

"With Frater, I learned how to give a man oral sex. How to suck the head of his cock really gently, and swirl my tongue around it. How to bite it, at an angle, with my teeth sinking into his little hole. How to run my tongue all the way down to his balls, and swallow those, one a time. How to keep rubbing his cock with my hand to make sure that he was stimulated enough to climax. Then how to make him feel good without actually swallowing, by letting his sperm shoot all over my face, and drip from my lips. I didn't have a taste for it, in those days—not like I do now!

"After we made love in the woods, Frater and I used to go back to the car naked, and we'd drive for miles through the hills with nothing on. He used to slip his hand between my legs while he was driving, and gently flick my clitoris. All that, and the wind blowing in my hair! And sometimes I'd put my head in his lap and suck his cock.

"Frater disappeared out of my life about as fast as he'd appeared. I missed him. You don't know how much I missed him. But I guess I always knew that it was one of those relationships that couldn't last. If it *had* lasted, Frater wouldn't have been Frater, and he wouldn't have been able to show me that sex is just sex, but romance and sex, that's an explosive combination.

"I went through three more relationships before I met Bruce. They were okay, but it was pretty apparent that my experience with Frater had made me too sexually swashbuckling for most men. They didn't like the idea of driving around nude, or making love in museums, which was another of Frater's favorites. A very nice guy called Morris asked me to marry him and I was very lonely at that particular time and I nearly said yes, but one night, after he had gone down on me and given me an orgasm by licking my pussy, I saw him in the bathroom scrubbing his face with a hot face cloth and furiously brushing his teeth. How unromantic can you be?

"I met Bruce when he came into my shop one lunchtime to buy a christening gift for his sister's baby. He's not classically good looking. He's big, well built, with short blond hair and a broken nose, but he has these soulful eyes that always make me melt. He was new in town—he'd just started a job with a local construction company— so he asked me if there was anyplace good where he could eat. I suggested somewhere, and then he asked me if I'd like to join him, and kind of fill him in on the local community. Our relationship started from there.

"He isn't a natural romantic, not like Frater. But he's a good lover, strong, and he always makes me feel small and feminine—which I like a lot, when you consider that I'm five-seven with shoulders like Xena the Warrior Princess and the bosom to match. The problem was that he was always so reserved, like he was holding back in case he made a fool of himself or committed himself too much. He never seemed to do anything spontaneous, and that included making love. Frater would try to have sex anywhere and everywhere. But you would never catch Bruce leaning you over a reading table in the local library, lifting up your skirt, pulling down your panties, and fucking you from behind; or sliding his hand up between your thighs in the middle of a performance of *The Magic Flute* and getting you so worked up that you had a damp patch on the back of your dress.

"I loved Bruce and I was sure that Bruce loved me. But he never did anything surprising or romantic and because *he* never did, I found that I was becoming the same. We showered, we went to bed, we kissed, we made love, we went to sleep. One night after we'd been making love I realized that this couldn't go on anymore. I wasn't exactly *bored*, but I was never ecstatic, either. A fuck was a fuck was a fuck, if you don't mind me misquoting Gertrude Stein. I needed Bruce to see that our relationship could be much more exciting. I've read a whole lot of your books and I know how wild some people's sex lives can be. Not only that, I needed my sex life with Bruce to be better than it was with Frater. I know that all of your women readers will understand that. I guess it doesn't matter so much if you've never known what it's like, having really exciting sex. But to have had it, and then to have lost it, and never to have sex as good as that again . . . I didn't want to be in that position, no way.

"It was January, and it had been snowing, but it was very still, and that gave me the inspiration for a winter fantasy. I always thought that *Dr. Zhivago* was so romantic—you know, all the furs and the Russian hats. I was expecting Bruce back around eight in the evening, so I went out into the yard and I arranged about fifty outdoor candles all around, and lit them. They looked really spectacular. Then I spread out our waterproof picnic sheet, and I heaped blankets on top of it, and on top of the blankets I laid two bearskin rugs that used to belong to my parents.

"I made myself into a fantasy Russian princess. I made up my eyes with sparkly silver. I wore my fur hat and my ankle-length foxfur coat and my black knee-length boots and a silver chain around my waist, and nothing else. Nothing else at all. I just managed to finish putting on my lip gloss when Bruce arrived home.

"I opened the door for him and he stood and stared at me and said, 'What's this?' I put on this thick Russian accent and went up to him and kissed him. I said, 'Velcome to my palace . . . my father, the tsar, has gone to St. Petersburg . . . my brothers have gone hunting . . . all of the servants are avay and ve can do vatever ve vish.'

"Bruce was laughing, but I didn't go out of character. I said, 'Come, Boris,' and led him through to the breakfast room. Outside, all the candles were shining and the trees were covered in snow and it looked absolutely magical.

"Bruce said, 'Are we having a party? Who's coming?'

"I took off his coat and loosened his necktie. I said, 'Only two people vill be coming, and that's you and me.' I poured him a glass of *krupnik*, which is Polish honey vodka, and I said, 'Here's to the greatest passion that ever was. *Nasdravye!*'

"He still didn't really understand what I was doing, but he played along all the same. I took the vodka bottle and I led him outside into the yard. There was no wind but it was still about ten below. I said, 'Tonight ve are going to celebrate the glorious revolution!' and I opened my fur coat so that he could see that I was naked. You can imagine how stiff my nipples were.

"I went up to him and I took off his sweater and unbuttoned his shirt. I kissed him and he kissed me back and this time his kisses were really greedy. I unbuckled his belt and pulled down his pants, and then his shorts, and his cock was already sticking up so hard. I knelt down to to help him take his shoes and his pants off, but when I stood up I had a handful of snow, and I pressed it right up between his legs. Then I rubbed his cock with it—really hard, so that it was freezing cold but glowing red. Then I knelt down and clamped my mouth around his cock to warm it up, and gave it a really lascivious licking.

"Now, Boris,' I told him. 'I am a princess and you have to do vatever I tell you. So, you must get into the bed and fuck me.'

"He didn't argue. He climbed in naked between the bearskins and I took off my coat and climbed in with him. He was shivering but I slid underneath him and kissed him and caressed him, pulling his cock, tugging at his balls, twisting his pubic hair around my fingers. I opened my legs and rubbed his cock up and down against my pussy so that he could feel how wet and warm it was. His cock was cold but it was totally one hundred ten percent hard. I don't think I'd ever known it so hard. His balls were all tight and wrinkled but that was probably the cold.

"He tried to push his cock into me but I gripped it tight and I would only let it in a little way. 'If I let you fuck me, what will you give me in return?' I asked him. He said, 'Everything. Anything. Just name it.' I said, 'You vill be my prince and you vill have half of my riches. But you vill have to fuck me every single night for a whole year, and every single night you vill have to think of a different way to do it.'

202

"He said, 'I promise. Every single night for a whole year.'

" 'And each time different?'

"He said, 'Yes, I swear it,' and it was then that I allowed his cock to slide through my hand into my pussy, until he was buried in it. He said, 'God, you're so warm inside.' And he started to fuck me . . . too fast at first. I squeezed my thighs together to slow him down and he got the message. He leaned forward while he was fucking me and kissed my face. My eyes, my cheeks, my nose, my lips. When he looked up he had silver sparkle all over his face, just like me, and it twinkled in the candlelight.

"It was incredible, fucking between those bearskins in that snowy, candlelit garden. I was really lost in my play-acting. I really did feel like a Russian princess. Bruce didn't say much, but he didn't do anything to break the spell. His loving was amazing. Like I said, he's very strong, and he really showed his strength. Once we were warmed up, he pulled back the bearskin and knelt upright. His cock was sticking up at a sharp angle, bright red and shining with juice. He lifted me up and lowered me onto it, and the feeling of chilled wet cock sliding up inside my pussy was sensational. It made he shiver so much that my teeth chattered.

"He fucked me like this for a while, kissing my breasts, sliding his hands down my back. He opened the cheeks of my ass and stroked my asshole with his fingertip, around and around. Then he actually stood up, and picked me up in his arms, with my legs entwined around his waist, and he fucked me harder than I've ever been fucked before. I was biting his shoulder because I could hardly stand the pleasure of it. My breasts were squashed against his chest, and my nipples were stiff with cold, and tingling, like your fingers when they start to thaw.

"His cock was driving so deep inside me that I gasped out loud every time he pushed it in. I clung onto him and his cock wouldn't stop ramming up between my legs and I seriously though that I was going to die from pleasure.

"After a while he laid me back down on the bearskin, and lay down beside me, and covered us both up. Although it was so cold, we were both sweating and panting. He lifted my leg and pushed his cock into me from the side, and fucked me slowly again—very, very slow—so that we both had the chance to catch our breath.

"I said, "The princess has a precious jewel . . . if you stroke it very gently you will please her greatly.' He touched my clitoris with his fingertip and began to stroke it so softly that I could hardly feel it, which is the way that really turns me on. It should feel tantalizing, you know, as if you want him to stroke it harder but he won't. Because if he strokes it too hard, it's just uncomfortable and it turns you off. But if he strokes it incredibly softly, hardly touching it at all, that builds up and builds up and in the end you can feel like your whole body is an orgasm just waiting to burst.

"It was starting to snow. Big, fluffy flakes dropping into my face and onto my hair. I said, 'The princess has another treasure, but it's hidden where you can't find it.' He got the message and started to stroke my asshole. I love that feeling. My idea of heaven would be to spend the whole afternoon face down on a silk couch, eating chocolates, while a stark naked Leonardo DiCaprio look-alike licked and fingered my asshole. Well, I can dream, can't I?

"Bruce pushed his fingertip into my asshole, and then more and more of his finger, until he was able to bend it inside me and feel his own cock inside my pussy. He stroked himself for a while, and then he pushed his finger even deeper into my ass, as deep as it could possibly go, and then he circled it around and around, on and on, until my ass began to feel like it was filled with ants, and I guess that was every nerve ending tickling me.

"There was just too much sensation. Bruce's finger right up inside my ass; his cock buried deep in my pussy; his finger stroking my clitoris. The feel of his skin against me, the feel of the bearskin rugs. The snow, the cold, the flickering candles. It was a fantasy come more than true. I closed my eyes tight and climaxed. There's no way to describe it. They talk about the earth moving, but they don't talk about the whole solar system exploding.

"When I was through shuddering and jumping and swearing, I threw back the bearskin rug so that we were both naked under the sky. Bruce wanted to take his finger out of me but I wouldn't let him. I took hold of his cock and rubbed it, while the snow came whirling down on top of us. He gritted his teeth and I knew that he was close to a climax because I could feel his finger curling up inside my ass. I paused, and held his cock gently so that I could feel it swell. He was right on the very edge of coming. His cock was actually pulsing and there was nothing he could do to stop it. I gave it one more rub and his sperm came leaping up out of it, three thick white jets of it, all over my fingers and all over his balls. I massaged his balls and his cock with it, and licked the snow from his face, and said, 'You have pleased your princess so much . . . tonight you can have more.' "

Did this spectacular piece of play-acting improve Helen's sexual relationship with Bruce? "The following evening he didn't make any mention of what had happened and by the time we went to bed I was beginning to think that maybe I'd made a fool of myself. But I was lying on top of the bed watching TV when Bruce came in and said, 'Is the princess ready for her treat?'

"I said, 'What treat?' but he said, in this hokey Russian accent, 'Close your eyes and you will find out.' I hate doing that, I hate closing my eyes, but I did. I felt him sit on the bed beside me. I felt him lift up my nightdress. and then I felt something cold slide down between the lips of my pussy, immediately followed by something warm. I opened my eyes and there was Bruce with a king-size popsicle. He was sliding it up and down between my legs and then licking me. He looked up and he laughed, and he said, 'What are you complaining about? You're a Russian princess. I thought you *liked* the cold!'

"Is it too much of a cliché if I say that my winter fantasy broke the ice between us?"

In the role of a Russian princess, Helen showed Bruce that she needed more from her sex life than he was giving her. Because it was all dressed up as a bit of play-acting, Bruce didn't feel that she was demeaning his sexual performance. In fact— as we've seen—he threw himself into the part of Boris with enthusiasm, and the play gave him some unusual ideas for future lovemaking.

The purpose of sexual play is to *inform* your partner rather than criticize, and to create a drama in which you can both indulge your erotic desires. Sexual play is a medium to promote closer understanding between you—a means of saying what you want without causing feelings of resentment or inadequacy. Many women find that it's a practical way of showing that they have much stronger and less conventional sexual appetites than their partners seem to suppose.

Karen, a 24-year-old magazine assistant from

New York, was pregnant with her first child by her lover Troy, a 28-year-old photographer. Karen's complaint was that ever since she found out she was pregnant, Troy treated her as if she were a piece of fragile china. He became extremely cautious about having sexual intercourse with her, and when he did "he was so gentle that I almost fell asleep." By the time she reached her sixth month, he was reluctant to give her orgasms because her stomach went so tight and hard when she climaxed, and he was afraid of precipitating a premature birth.

"You can't how imagine how frustrated I was," said Karen. "I was feeling sexier than I had ever felt before. My hair was shiny, my face was glowing. I was in perfect health and my gynecologist had told me that it was perfectly safe to continue making love right up until term, so long as I didn't do anything stupid.

"I was having sexual fantasies like nothing I'd ever had before. I couldn't describe them—well, not all of them, they were just so kinky. I used to take a rest every afternoon and while I was resting I couldn't stop these ideas from coming into my head. I mean, they were truly filthy, some of them. Look at me, I'm still blushing now. I started to think that I must be perverted or something. But I kept thinking about them day after day, and in the end I couldn't help myself from masturbating. I used to masturbate every afternoon—sometimes using my fingers and sometimes using a dildo, too, which Troy didn't even know that I had. I was always careful not to push it in too far, and I always made sure it was scrupulously clean.

"I told one of my best friends that I was having these fantasies all the time and that I was kind of worried about them. But she said that when she was pregnant her fantasies had become so way out that she was thinking of going to confession.

"She said it was nothing to worry about. She had talked to her doctor, who had told her that it was extremely common. Like, your hormones are going at full blast, but at the same time you're not getting very much sex. A lot of the time you're too *tired* for sex, especially if you have to wait for your lover to come home at night."

And what had her friend's doctor advised? "She told my friend to try yoga. Empty her mind. Try to think of something else, apart from sex. Like fields full of flowers; or the ocean breaking on the shore. She said that a pregnancy was a physical celebration of the wonders of a woman's body, and she shouldn't let her sexual feelings distract her."

I personally don't believe that making love with the father of your unborn child is any kind of distraction from the wonder of pregnancy; and I certainly don't think that trying to picture the ocean breaking on the shore is much of a substitute for sexual satisfaction. Of course I advise caution during pregnancy, and if you have any doubts whatsoever you should always consult your gynecologist, but in a normal pregnancy there is no reason why you shouldn't continue having sex until you're almost ready to give birth.

There are some compelling reasons why you *should* continue to have regular sex. It can ease your own sexual frustration and it can help to remind you that you are still an attractive woman in your own right and not just a "vessel" for the baby inside you. Equally important, it can bring you very physically close to your lover, at a time when the baby is already beginning to make itself felt as a divisive factor in your sex life.

It isn't surprising that such a high percentage of men commit adultery during and immediately after their partners' pregnancy.

I suggested to Karen that she should try to play out her sexual fantasies for real. All right, they were more extreme than any fantasies she'd ever had before, and there was no doubt that this was partly attributable to the psychological and physiological changes that occur in pregnancy. But all the same, they would certainly excite Troy, and they would give him a mental "library" of very powerful erotic images of her. This "library" would help to maintain his sexual interest in her at a high level in the difficult months to come, when most of her energy and her attention would be focused on the baby, and Troy would be feeling slightly left out in the cold. Even the most devoted father occasionally feels jealous that his lover suddenly seems to have eyes for nobody but the new kid on the block.

Troy could even assist his memory by taking photographs or videos.

Karen said, "I knew exactly what part I wanted to play. I wanted to be a dominatrix. All leather straps and whips, like Madonna. Most of my fantasies were about having two or three men, and making them do whatever I wanted them to do. I found a mail order catalog that sold every kind of S&M outfit and accessory that you could think of. I couldn't wear a tight leather corset or anything like that, because I was so pregnant. But I ordered a harness made of black leather belts and buckles and studs, and a black leather hood, and a cat-o'-nine-tails whip that had a black rubber dildo for a handle. I also ordered some black leather wrist and ankle bands.

"Everything arrived when Troy was at work, so I was able to try them on. The harness was very erotic. It had two circular pieces of leather for my breasts to fit through, and then four thin straps holding a metal nipple-ring in place. My breasts were enormous, and my nipples poked through the rings like two big strawberries. Three more straps went down between my legs, two at the front and one at the back, but they left my cunt completely exposed.

"I put on a pair of little black high-heeled boots, and then I put on the mask. That was really strange. Very erotic, but really strange. It covered my head completely, with two eye-holes, two nostril-holes, and a mouth with a zipper across it. It fastened around the neck with a buckle, and it had a kind of plume of top made out of strips of leather, like a whip.

"Once I'd put it on I paraded in front of the mirror. In a way, I frightened myself, because this was very weird stuff, and it stirred up all kinds of sexual feelings in me that I hardly dared to think about. It felt *forbidden,* if you can follow what I mean, especially since I was pregnant. But I was so turned on that my cunt was almost dripping. I sat on a kitchen chair in front of the mirror and I masturbated, imagining that I had ordered a slave girl to masturbate, and that I was watching her. I opened my cunt wide and rubbed my clitoris with my thumb, which is what I always like to do. My cunt was very swollen anyway, and it looked all plump and juicy, like a pink grapefruit that somebody had just split open. I slipped two fingers into my cunt hole, and I rubbed my clitoris quicker and quicker, and it only took me a couple of minutes before I had an orgasm. My stomach went as hard as a football. But I lay down afterward and rested and when my stomach began to relax I felt a good warm feeling come over me.

"I didn't wear the harness that evening when

Troy came home because I knew that I'd be too tired. I saved it for the weekend. He was still lying in bed asleep on Saturday morning when I put on the harness and the boots and the hood. I came into the bedroom and flicked his shoulder with the cat-o'-nine-tails. He waved his hand and didn't even open his eyes. He must have thought it was a fly. So I flicked him harder, and this time the whip really cracked. He sat bolt upright in bed and said, 'Karen? What the hell's going on?'

"I said, 'You've been bad, haven't you? I have to punish you.'

"He laughed. He said, 'You have to punish me? What have I done?'

"I said, 'You've been going around making girls pregnant. You're going to suffer for that.'

"He threw back the covers and started to get out of bed but I flicked at his cock with my whip, and caught him right on the tip of it. He said, 'Ow!' and covered himself up with both hands. I said, 'If you don't do what I tell you to do, you'll get worse than that.'

"I told him to lie facedown on the bed, with his hands behind him. He was great, he entered right into the spirit of what I was doing. He even started improvising, saying, 'Don't hurt me. I promise I won't make any more girls pregnant. Please, don't hurt me.'

"I slipped the wrist bands on him, buckled them tight, and then clipped them both together, so that he was handcuffed. I made him open his legs a little way, and I put my hand down between them and fondled his big soft balls. Then I gave him a lash with the cat-o'-nine-tails—not very hard, but enough to make him clench the cheeks of his ass and leave some thin red stripes across it. 'Are you sorry yet?' I asked him.

"He said, 'Yes, yes. I'm sorry. Don't hurt me.' I said, 'I don't believe you,' and I whipped him again, harder this time. I gave him six lashes altogether, and his ass was covered in criss-cross marks. I said, 'That's your punishment for treating girls so badly. Now you've got to prove that you'll never do it again.' He said, 'I won't, I won't, I promise you.' But I pulled the zipper across my mouth to show him that I wasn't going to discuss it. I took a bottle of hand lotion out of my dressing-table drawer and I squeezed a whole lot into the palm of my hand. Then I smeared it in between the cheeks of his ass, and poked my finger into his asshole to make sure that it was properly lubricated. I turned the whip around and pushed the black dildo handle into his asshole. The dildo had a little smiling Chinese face on the head, and it disappeared completely into Troy's tight red ring. I pulled it out a little way, then slid it all the way up, all six inches of it. He winced, but he didn't complain. When I pulled it out and pushed it back in a second time, his asshole was wide open and ready for it . . . and that was actually the first time I realized how much men enjoy being fucked up the ass. Not necessarily by other men, you know, but with dildoes and vibrators and carrots and stuff like that.

"I rolled Troy over, with the dildo still stuck up inside him. His cock was totally hard. I tugged open the zipper in my mask, and took his cock into my mouth. I sucked him and gently chewed him for a while, and then licked all the way down his cock to his balls. Then I said, 'That's enough. You have to fuck me now, so that I know you won't ever fuck anybody else."

"He said, 'I promise. I promise I won't ever fuck anybody else.'

"I slowly pulled the whip-handle out of his ass. But then I took the leather braids and I wound them around his cock and his balls and tied them tight. I said, 'You have to fuck me now, but first I have to go to the bathroom, and you're coming with me.' I tugged the cat-o'-nine-tails and of course he had to follow me into the bathroom or risk having his cock stretched!

"What I did then was to act out one of my dirtiest fantasies. Right up to the moment I did it, I wasn't sure that I was going to have the nerve. But in my harness and my leather mask, I felt like a different person. Very dominant. And being pregnant made me feel even stronger. I'm not quite sure what you'd call it. Confident? But more than confident; self-possessed.

"I sat on the bidet and made Troy kneel on the tiled floor in front of me. I opened my legs wide and opened up my cunt with my fingers. I took hold of his hair with my other hand and forced his head down in front of me. 'You know what you have to do now?' I told him. 'You have to wash your face.' I was so sexually aroused that I was panting, and when I tried to pee it came only in short, sharp bursts. But I took three or four really deep breaths, and I relaxed, and then it suddenly gushed out of me. It splashed into the bidet and right up into Troy's face. I pulled him closer and said, 'Come on, open your mouth, you must be thirsty.' He opened his mouth wide and I peed straight into his tongue. He was swallowing some of it but a lot was pouring down his chin. He took a mouthful and then he spouted it back out again, so that it splashed against my cunt.

"We had never tried wet sex before. I don't know whether Troy had ever done it with anybody, but for me it was just a dirty fantasy that I had never dared to tell him about. And here we were, actually doing it; and you should have seen Troy's face, it was like he was in seventh heaven.

"When I was finished, I said 'Stand up,' and tugged at the whip. He stood up in front of me with the black braids all laced around his cock and his cock was really straining. I said, 'Aren't you going to give me the same pleasure that I gave you?'

'I held his cock in my hand and squeezed it hard. It took him a moment of effort, but without warning he started to pee, too. It was warm and glittering and pungent. I streamed right out of the end of his cock all over my breasts. I waved his cock from side to side, from one nipple to the other. That's a sensation like nothing else in the world, especially when you're pregnant and your nipples are extra-sensitive. Then he peed all over my swollen stomach, so it ran down between my legs, and in the end I pulled him down into a crouch so that he was peeing right up against my clitoris at point-blank range. Ohh . . . that felt amazing.

"We went back into the bedroom. I unfastened Troy's wrist bands and then I lay on the bed and he climbed on top of me. We were still wet, still sticky, but that added to the excitement of it, the feeling that we were doing something dirty. I was so excited that I started to have an orgasm almost as soon as Troy pushed his cock inside me. I went rigid, and I had a spasm every time he went in and out. It didn't take long for him to climax, either. He jolted once, and then again, and then again, and I was sure that I could feel his sperm filling me up inside.

"Afterward we lay back for a long time and stroked each other and talked. Troy said, 'That's a side of you I've never seen before.' I said, 'That's because I've never shown it to anybody before.' It turned out that he'd had fantasies about pretty much the same kind of thing; but of course it isn't something you talk about, even to your lover.

"Last summer, after the baby was born, we went in for a lot of wet sex. We used to do it in the orchard of this house we rented on Cape Cod; I used to take a swallow of pee and then a bite of apple. Sometimes we did in on the beach if we could get the privacy . . . you can dash into the sea afterward and wash yourself off. It's a very playful, intimate thing. It's childish, in a way. It's like doing something really, really naughty when you're a kid, and that's what makes it so exciting. We don't do it much anymore, if ever. I guess we've grown out of it. But our sex life is very much closer now because we're aware that we both have pretty extreme fantasies, and we're not afraid to talk about them, even if we don't often try them out. And there's one thing I know . . . that when I get pregnant again, if I ever do, Troy will make sure that I get all the sex I need."

You'll notice that during her wet sex session with Troy, Karen made sure that she didn't swallow. As I've discussed before in earlier books, the fresh urine of a healthy person is completely sterile, and you won't come to any harm if you happen to ingest a limited quantity. Some people swear that urine has beneficial properties, and regularly drink a glass of their own midflow urine every morning. However most doctors agree that if there was something in urine that made it worth drinking, your body would have absorbed it the first time around.

Karen said about her sexual fantasies that "we're not afraid to talk about them, even if we don't often try them out," and this, to me, is one of the most positive after-effects of her sexual play. If you have a particular fantasy, it can be almost as arousing to explain it to your partner as it is to act it out. In any case, some of your more extreme fantasies—even if they seem mind-blowingly stimulating when you *think* about them—would be far too uncomfortable, far too painful, and far too repulsive to perform in real life. That doesn't mean that you should be ashamed of them, or that you shouldn't discuss them with your partner. Everybody has sexual fantasies, some of them blushingly disgusting. It is simply up to you to decide which of those fantasies might happily enliven your love life if you play it for real.

Readers send me countless letters asking my advice on all kinds of fantastic sexual acts. One woman wanted to know if it would distress her goldfish if she were to insert it into her vagina during masturbation. (Answer: yes.) Another asked me to recommend a diet that would make her feces more attractive—her partner was aroused by the idea of her excreting while they made love. (Answer: Swiss muesli, milk chocolate, and edible flowers.) Still another wanted to know if it were physically possible for four men to enter one woman, vaginally and anally, all the same time. (Answer: yes, provided they do it in the correct order, so that their ten legs don't become hopelessly entangled, and so that the last entrant can be given assistance by his fellows into the tightest remaining orifice.)

One of the most frequently asked questions is about homosexuality. So many women write and say that they find themselves wondering what it would be like to make love to another woman ("I keep thinking what it might be like to fondle another woman's breasts and to kiss another woman's vagina. I imagine that it would taste like diluted honey.") And I get the same from men. ("I'm heterosexual, married, two children, but the other day I saw a muscular young man changing on the beach and I glimpsed his cock . . . to my bewilderment, I found myself having a fleeting fantasy about taking it into my mouth and sucking it.")

Our sexual characters are highly complex and we rarely get the opportunity (if ever) to discuss our urges openly. This is a pity, because it can cause a great deal of anxiety, self-doubt, and self-disgust. It is quite common for people of both sexes to have homosexual fantasies—just as it is perfectly normal for people of both sexes to be aroused by homosexual pornography of both sexes. Men are stimulated by seeing acts of lesbianism and women are excited by seeing acts of male homosexuality. One famous actress is known to have quite an appetite for watching men having anal intercourse.

Because we have sexual fantasies, however, that doesn't mean that we're ever going to act them out. Or even if we do—for the benefit of livening up our sex lives, or for our own sexual curiosity—that doesn't necessarily mean we're certified sadists or masochists or homosexuals or whatever. You may feel the urge to try a broccoli omelet but that doesn't mean you're a closet vegetarian. Karen fantasized about whipping Troy and she even played at whipping him for real but that didn't make her a sadist—just as the father of two who daydreamed about sucking a young man's penis wasn't a homosexual.

I have no way of telling if my readers are serious about attempting these sexual variations, or whether they are simply using their inquiries as a way of explaining their fantasies with somebody else. Quite often, the act of talking or writing about your private urges to somebody else is enough to satisfy them. That's why, even if you don't feel that you can demonstrate your sexual needs to your partner in the form of role-playing, you should at least try to find a way to discuss them.

Mind you, there are plenty of ways in which you can use sexual play to have a whole lot of fun, and reveal at the same time what your sexual urges are.

7

Dice Girls Finish First

In the British Museum there is a Greek mirror dating back to 350 B.C. showing a bare-breasted goddess of love, Aphrodite, playing a game of knuckle bone with the great god Pan. It may predate strip poker by 2,000 years, but men and women have been playing games of chance since the days of Ancient Egypt, and gaming and sex have always been inextricably intertwined.

It's not just the money, although large amounts of money have a sexual attraction all their own. Gaming is "to risk anything of value on a game of chance," and sexual favors are as valuable as money or property or shiny new automobiles. Throughout the centuries, games of chance have been played for the permanent or temporary ownership of slave women, concubines, girlfriends, and wives—not to forget, of course, the removal of blouses, bras, and panties.

Not only that, gaming does have an underlying sexual element. Many addictive gamblers have described the sensation of placing a huge and risky bet as "erotic." The famous Russian novelist Fyodor Dostoyevsky, of *Crime and Punishment* fame, was so obsessed by gambling that he ejaculated in his pants when he lost a large sum of money at roulette.

The kind of sexual gaming that can enhance your love life is not nearly as serious as Mr. Dostoyevsky's, although you should ultimately get an orgasm out of it, just as he did.

Playing games with your partner for sexual stakes can introduce a great deal of fun and laughter into your love life. It can also make it very much easier for you to suggest some lively variations, *without* making it seem that you're complaining that your bedtimes are becoming just a little bit too predictable.

You can play any game of chance or skill, from spoof to backgammon, depending on how quickly you want to have sex. If you're in no special hurry, you could even put a bet on a game of chess, or who can be first to finish a cryptic crossword. The most important thing is to choose a game at which you're pretty evenly matched, and a game that you both really enjoy. I don't recommend Monopoly, which is notorious for causing serious domestic friction. All the same, I came across one couple who had devised their own version of Erotic Monopoly, changing certain buildings and streets into bordellos and red-light districts that—when acquired—would entitle them to a brief act of sexual play. If the man bought Fifth Avenue, his partner would take off her panties and give him a quick feel up her skirt, Fifth Avenue being the haunt of women with "fur coats and no panties." If either of them went to jail, they have to allow their partner to subject them to a strip search. The winner would be able to say when, where, and how they were going to make love—but they would have to pay for it using their remaining Monopoly money.

There are many different ways in which you can use small flirtatious pleasures during the course of a game to increase the erotic tension. Kelly, a 23-year-old salesgirl from Birmingham, Alabama, plays checkers with her boyfriend Redmond, 25, a game that can hardly be described as having much in the way of sexual charisma. But the way they play it, it almost scorches the board.

"Every time we take one of each other's men, we say what we want the other person to do to us if we win. Like, I'll say to Redmond, 'You'll have to pour maple syrup on my nipples and suck it all off.' Or Redmond will say to me, 'You'll have to pour baby oil in your cleavage and squeeze my cock in between your breasts.' It's very sexy and it's a whole lot of fun because you have to keep on thinking up these amazing things you want the other person to do to you. We make it a strict rule that you can never say the same thing twice. It really stretches your imagination, not to mention a few other places!

"We play three games and whoever wins the best of three gets to have everything done to them. Some of the suggestions are almost impossible, but we always end up laughing and having a great time. And we always end up having a really good fuck, too.

"Redmond won a couple of nights ago. I had to take off all of my clothes and undress him with my teeth. Fortunately he was wearing a T-shirt so I didn't have any buttons to unfasten, and his belt buckle was pretty chunky so that wasn't too difficult. I had to tug down his zipper with my teeth and that was a problem because his cock was bulging so much. I managed it, though, and he always wears boxer shorts, and they came down easily. His cock was so hard that it felt like it was carved out of mahogany, and his balls were all wrinkled and tight, like walnuts.

"I had to massage him all over with baby oil, using my body instead of my hands. Then I had to push fifteen grapes into my vagina and sit astride his face while he ate them out of me. He kept licking my clitoris while he was doing that, and I was dying for him to carry on, but *he* was the one who had won the game, and so I had to do whatever he wanted me to do. If you cheat, or if you refuse to do something, or if you do something half-heartedly, there's not nearly so much fun in it.

"Once he'd eaten all the grapes, I had to turn around and crouch on top of him, licking his cock like it was a Popsicle. At the same time he pushed a long plastic bead necklace into my asshole, bead by bead. I never mind him doing that, it feels sensational. When he was finished, I had to turn around and sit on his cock, and slowly ride up and down on it until he warned me that he was close to coming. Then I had to climb off him— even though I didn't really want to—and suck his cock until he came, and swallow it. But after that I had to lie on my back with my legs wide open while he went down on me and licked me to a climax, too. And when I was climaxing, I had to pull the bead necklace slowly out of my ass and wind it around his cock and his balls.

"When we were through making love, I had to go the icebox and bring out a carton of rocky road and we sat naked together and ate it with our fingers and smeared it all over each other, and in the end we made love all over again. It was great, I can tell you. But when I win, I make him do the same kind of things to me. Last summer I made him go down on me underwater when I was standing in the swimming pool. Another time I made him wear stockings and a garter belt and a pair of my panties while he was making love to me. It's only a game, but it makes our sex life so much more fun, you know, because we're always trying to outdo each other—always trying to think of more inventive ways to turn each other on. Once I made Redmond wear crocodile clips on his nipples, and another time I pushed a Snickers bar right up my asshole and he had to eat it out of me. I don't know what anybody would have thought if they had burst into the bedroom and caught us.

"What I enjoy about a game like this is that you're always thinking up new ways of pleasing *yourself*, so if you win your partner knows that you're really going to get a thrill out of what he's doing to you, and vice versa.

"If you didn't have a game like this, how would you ask your partner to do anything out of the ordinary? You couldn't just sit down one evening and say, 'Darling, I want you to shave your pussy and then allow me to masturbate you with a giant cucumber,' could you? But a game gives you the license to do that, doesn't it? It allows you to try so much wild and wonderful sex play without feeling embarrassed."

As a side issue, I was interested when Kelly mentioned that removing her pubic hair was one of the first demands that Redmond had made . . . and now she made a point of staying "bare down there." Over twenty-five years ago, when I was still editor of both *Penthouse* and *Penthouse Forum*, I carried out an informal but extensive survey to find out how men imagined "the woman of their dreams." Apart from the expected answers, such as large breasts and long legs, I was surprised to see how many of them mentioned a shaved pubis. I repeated the research when I was preparing my first book, *How to Drive Your Man Wild in Bed*, with similar results. and this was at a time when the raunchiest of men's magazines weren't allowed to show even a discreet tuft of pubic hair, let alone openly exposed genitals.

I suggested to women who wanted to surprise and please their lovers that they try shaving their pubic hair, and the response was instantaneous. I have a letter from 1977, in which Sandy from Pittsburgh tells me that her husband "went really wild when he saw that I'd shaved my pussy. He lifted me out of the tub and carried me through to the bedroom and made love to me then and there, for the first time in nearly two weeks. And after that he couldn't leave me alone. He loves it. He's always looking at it, touching me, fondling me, and making love me. I think he's had a permanent hard-on ever since I did it."

June, a 34-year-old homemaker from Tallahassee, Florida, wrote in 1978 to say that shaving had changed her husband's attitude toward her overnight. "I think he must always have had the impression that I wasn't very interested in sex. The trouble is that I've never really been very demonstrative in bed. I've never known what to do. But when he saw me in front of the mirror that evening it was like he'd been struck by lightning. I said, 'Do you like it?' and all he could do was nod, and keep on nodding."

As I've said so many times before, men are very quickly aroused by visual stimuli, and the sight of a woman's exposed vulva is arguably the strongest visual stimulus of all. By removing your pubic hair, you're flirting with your lover in the most unequivocal way possible. You're showing him quite plainly and openly that you want to have sex with him. It's the female equivalent of walking around with an erect penis.

Of course, many women depilate simply because they find it more aesthetically pleasing, especially with today's high-cut panties and swimwear. But New York's most popular waxing salon, the J International salon on West 57th Street, reports that it is booked solid for the whole week before Valentine's Day. The J salon is run by six Brazilian sisters whose names all begin with J, and they are responsible for what is now known as "the Brazilian bikini wax" or "the thong wax" or "the *Playboy* wax." This goes well beyond the trimming of yesteryear, which removed only those hairs that strayed outside the bikini line, and instead involves removing all pubic hair, except for those women who like a tiny decorative tuft on their *mons veneris*.

Supermodel Naomi Campbell is a regular client.

"The Brazilian wax is great because it cleans everything away. The business I'm in, I need to do that and I'm supposed to do that. They don't ask me to do that, but I just feel free to do it on my own. It's just how I like to be." Actress Kirstie Alley is another J salon customer.

Linda Wells, editor-in-chief of *Allure* magazine, agrees that women are doing it just because it's sexy. "People are always talking about women wearing sexy lingerie, but this takes it one step further."

Removing pubic hair as a way of arousing men goes back a long, long way. The Hindu temples built around the 9th and 10th centuries A.D. are covered with bas-relief sculptures of women openly showing their sexual organs. Philip Rawson, the curator of the Gulbenkian Museum of Oriental art, wrote, "The feminine vulva is freely offered to view as a beauty with an expression of its own. The clitoris is often much in evidence. In Orissa, for example, the vulva's openness proclaims the women's eager nature. Elsewhere, as at Khajuraho, its frontal presentation serves as a mark of desirable youth. But another reason for it being visible is that in India it was always usual for women to depilate their pubic region. Special thumb rings, with mirrors inset, were used for this purpose."

These days, it is rare to see a model in a man's magazine who hasn't completely shaved or trimmed her pubic hair, but more and more ordinary women are doing it as part of their normal hair-skin-manicure routine. Jeanne, 31, an executive for a secretarial employment agency, said, "I started doing it three or four years ago, and now I always do it as a matter of routine. I like it. It feels cleaner and fresher somehow. And my partner never tires of it. I keep trying to persuade him to shave off *his* hair, too, because one of my friends said that her boyfriend had done it, and that fully hairless sex is absolutely the most erotic experience in the world. Unfortunately, he's kind of reluctant. He's allowed me to trim it short with nail scissors, and I got him to shave the long hairs off his balls . . . I said that I would never suck them again, if he didn't. But so far he hasn't agreed to go the whole way."

Jeanne might have been able to persuade her boyfriend if she had included shaving in a sexual game of chance. Sheena, 29, an agricultural technician from Cedar Rapids, Iowa, said that she had been able to persuade her 33-year-old partner Damon to do "almost anything" since they had started to play an erotic version of the word game Scrabble. "We were both Scrabble enthusiasts before we met, and so there's always been this hot sense of competition between us, even though we're lovers. Who can score the most points with the shortest word, which of us can come up with a word that the other has never heard of, that kind of thing. We always used to have a stake. Maybe the loser has to take the winner out for a pizza, or the loser has to buy a bottle of champagne. We get pretty passionate about it sometimes, especially if one of us suspects the other one of cheating! I refused to make love to Damon one night because he cheated. He made up this word 'yryx' and pretended it was an African antelope.

"We call our game Sexy Scrabble. We got into it one evening after we'd had an argument about who was going to use the car the next day. Damon had his way, as usual. But when we were playing Scrabble that evening, I managed to spell out the words "selfish" and "prick" right next to each other. In reply, he put down "sorry" and "asshole." We laughed like crazy and then we kissed and made up. We kissed and made up so much we abandoned the game and went to bed, and we were so hot for it that Damon didn't even take my panties off. He gave me a beautiful fucking, even though he still wouldn't agree to give me the car!

"Afterward, though, we were lying on the bed, and Damon said, 'Why don't we see if we can finish a game of Scrabble using nothing but sexy words?' I said sure. It wouldn't be easy, and it would need a lot of skill and a very racy vocabulary! We both agreed that we had to have a stake, but it had to have something to do with sex. So in the end we agreed that each of us would write a sexual act on a card, and whoever won, they would get to perform this sexual act, or have it performed on them, depending on what it was.

"We didn't play the first game right away because some friends came over and we had to jump out of bed and straighten ourselves up and pretend that we hadn't just been fucking! But we had a free evening on Friday and I brought home some beautiful *tagliatelle vongole* and Damon brought a couple of bottles of Chianti, and after we'd eaten we sat on the floor and set out the Scrabble board. We each wrote our stake on a slip of paper, folded it, and passed it over. The rules were whoever won, the other had to do whatever it said on that slip of paper, immediately, willingly, and without any argument whatsoever.

"I couldn't guess what Damon had written on his slip and I don't think he could guess what was on mine. Part of the thrill of the game is that you don't know what's going to happen to you if you lose. It may be something really erotic and exciting. It may be something terrible. But whatever it is, you're not allowed to say no. And you think *you've* seen tense games of Scrabble before!

"What made it harder was that we were only allowed to use sexual words. They could be colloquial or medical. They could be slang. They could even be foreign. The only thing they couldn't be was a proper noun. Like, you could have "masochism" but you couldn't have "masoch," the guy they named it after.

"The game was terrific. At first we were beating our brains trying to come up with sexual words, but you'd be surprised how many there are. "Come" was allowed, by the way. So was "poon-tang" and "pecker." But we had high-falultin' words, too, like "zoophiliacs," who are people who love animals just a little too much; and "het-aera," who were courtesans in Ancient Greece.

"I won the first game and when Damon opened my slip he saw what I wanted him to do. Take off all of his clothes, tie a scarf around his eyes as a blindfold, and go on licking my cunt until I had at least two orgasms. He didn't mind that at all, because I expected him to do it in the sixty-nine position so that I could lick his cock at the same time. I wasn't going to let him have all the fun. It took him a long time, but he did it, and because he had to give me *two* orgasms he really concentrated on his technique, gently pulling my cunt lips apart so that my clitoris stood out proud, and swirling his tongue around it, which felt out of this world. Afterward, I let him make love to me, but I made him keep his blindfold on. He said that when he was making love to me he could visualize me better in his head than he could if he could actually see."

Sheena raises an interesting point about love-making when you're blindfold. I've talked to many people of both sexes who prefer to make love in the dark—not because they're shy or because they're ashamed of their physical appearance, but because they find that it helps them to create what you might describe as a "sensual map" in their minds. They are guided by their partner's responses rather than the sight of their breasts or their genitals, and they often find that they can give their partner a much more sensual experience by stroking their backs, or their sides, or licking the soles of their feet. Making love in the dark can make it easier for you to feel that you are physically and emotionally joined together, because there are no visual boundaries between you. Even that supreme visual stimulus that we've just been discussing, the shaven vulva, can take on a highly erotic identity after lights out. As Bernard, a 37-year-old lawyer from San Diego, California, remarked, "There is nothing more sensual than licking the completely hairless cunt of somebody you love in total darkness. Nothing. If somebody could open a theme park based on that experience alone, they'd make a fortune."

Back at the Scrabble game, Sheena and David continued to play each other for sexual favors, and their knowledge of sex and sexuality grew enormously as they researched new words to fit on their Scrabble board. "Even if it wasn't so sexy, and if it wasn't such fun, it's certainly proved to be an education."

Both of them learned hitherto undisclosed secrets about each other's sexual urges. When she lost the second game, Sheena was surprised (and a little shocked) to discover that Damon wanted to have anal intercourse with her, which they had never had before.

"I wasn't sure about it at all. I nearly refused. But then I thought that thousands of other women do it. A close friend of mine said she always did it whenever she had a period, and she's one of the most composed and elegant women you could ever meet. So I thought *well, Damon must have had it on his mind, and if he wants to do it so much, I can at least try.*

"We showered and went to bed and Damon was very tender and understanding, but at the same time I knew that he wasn't going to let me off the hook. He kissed me and caressed my breasts and took a long time stroking me and touching me and making me feel aroused. He gently played with my clitoris and slipped his finger into my cunt, and I was beginning to think that he was going to make love to me in the normal way. But then he produced a tube of KY jelly from beside the bed and squeezed a whole lot all over the head of his cock. He massaged it all down the shaft, and then he slid his slippery fingers in between the cheeks of my ass.

"I wasn't exactly frightened, but I didn't know what to expect, and I was worried that it would hurt me. After all, his cock was enormous, and standing up like a pillar, and my asshole is only a tiny little ring. He lay close behind me, and slipped one finger into my asshole. My muscles gripped it tight. But he kissed my ear and shushed me, and told me to relax. All I had to do was push his finger out, that's what he said. Push it out, just like going to the john. I pushed, but of course that opened my asshole wider, and so he was able to work his finger even further in. He stroked the inside of my ass, and I wasn't sure whether I liked the feeling or not. It was sexy, but it was a bit too much like wanting to go the bathroom at the same time.

"Next he drew out his finger and I could feel the head of his cock up against my asshole. Everything was slippery with KY ... his cock, his fingers, my ass cheeks, my thighs. He said, very quietly, Push against me ... don't let me in.' I pushed against him and then I felt the head of his cock right inside my asshole, stretching it wide. My first reaction was to clench my muscles again, and I almost squeezed him out again. But then he said, 'Push again,' and I pushed, and his cock went even further in. It felt enormous, and my natural reaction was still to squeeze it out of me. But he pushed it deeper, and deeper, and I felt myself opening up ... I felt myself *wanting* to open up, wanting to have this huge hard cock right up inside my ass, deeper and deeper. Gradually I managed to stop myself from squeezing it, even though I couldn't help an occasional spasm. Damon was stroking my clitoris at the same time, and the good feeling in my ass began to grow and grow.

"Damon reached across to the nightstand and took hold of my hand mirror. He said, 'Raise your leg ... now look. Isn't that fantastic?' I looked down and I could see my cunt, my labia wide open. And then I saw my asshole, shiny and scarlet and stretched tight around this massive dark cock, sunk so deep inside me, right up to the balls. He said, 'Watch,' and he slowly drew his cock out of me, right out, and my asshole remained open, flaming red. He plunged his cock back in again so that I could watch it disappear inside me, and by this time I was so turned on that I didn't resist at all, and I didn't feel the slightest pain.

"He was incredibly tender. I felt like a virgin in the hands of a really experienced lover, and I suppose I was. All the time he was fucking my ass he was stroking my clitoris, and after a while I began to realize that I was going to have an orgasm and there was nothing I could do to stop it. I wanted him inside me when that happened, I wanted him deep inside me. So I reached around and dug my nails into his thigh and held him where he was.

"Then my whole ass went into these big waves of muscular spasm, and I literally blacked out for a second. The spasms were so strong that I literally forced Damon right out of me. But he knelt up, and opened my legs, and started rubbing his cock, really fast and hard. It only took him about ten seconds to reach a climax. All of this thick white sperm came shooting out of his cock, and he aimed it right into my asshole, which was still wide open. Most of it went inside, but some of it splashed onto my cunt, and another squirt went up my thigh.

"I felt like we'd both become so much closer in our sexual relationship, like we'd broken a barrier, and now we could do anything together, absolutely anything. I don't think Damon would have minded if I'd told him that I never wanted to have anal intercourse again. I can imagine that there are some women who don't like it at all, and that's their prerogative, isn't it? We still would have broken that barrier, we still would have taken that step. Like, he asked me to do something that he'd always wanted to do, but hadn't had the nerve; and I said yes. That was what the step was and I know a whole lot of couples who have never taken that step, and never will. Maybe they feel fulfilled enough as they are. I hope they do. But the sex that Damon and I are having together these days . . . I never thought that it was possible.

"Fortunately for Damon, I love anal sex. I never realized what I'd been missing. If you really want a cock up your ass, you can take it just as easy as taking it up your cunt. You can use a whole lot of other things up your ass, too, like vibrators and love eggs. Once Damon shook up a bottle of chilled sparkling wine. He pushed it up my ass and gave me a champagne enema! You haven't lived until you've tried that!

"We've tried all sorts of other sexual variations, like tying each other up and having sex in the open air. We made love in the pouring rain once, totally naked, and that was outstanding.

"I don't think we would have progressed nearly so far in our sex life if we hadn't played Sexual Scrabble. It was a way of telling each other what we wanted. You know, a way of spelling out the things that, otherwise, we wouldn't have had the words for."

Occasionally, games are used by more than one couple as a way of breaking the ice at a group sex party. The most basic of these are Spin-the-Bottle to decide who's going to pair off with whom, and the good old car-key Lucky Dip. But I've come across outwardly conservative people who use bridge as a prelude to orgies, with the losing pair having to perform sexually in front of the winning pair, and doing everything that the winning pair directs them to do—and that means *everything*. Inevitably, I was told, the winning pair join in with the losing pair, so the game becomes a sexual free-for-all.

Strip poker still seems to be reasonably popular, especially among younger people, although it seems to be played mostly for incidental titillation than it is as a prelude to full-scale sex. I spoke to some New York college students about strip poker and they told me that while they enjoyed playing it now and again, they were usually too drunk by the end of the game to worry about having their wicked way with anybody.

One group of friends from Phoenix, Arizona, however, found that a game of Trivial Pursuit was a novel way to overcome their inhibitions and explore the outer limits of sexual pleasure. Sally, 24, a print shop designer, had been friends since college with Perri, 25. Sally was dating Kenneth, 28, and Perri was introduced to Kenneth's best friend, Charles, who was 26.

"Kenneth and me had a very steady relationship," said Sally. "He was very quiet, very calm, very dependable. A lot of my friends said that meeting Kenneth was the best thing that had ever happened to me, because I used to be so wild and go out with so many boys . . . some of whom were not exactly the type you'd be brave enough to bring home to meet your parents. There was one guy who was kind of a biker, called Snake. He looked real frightening, with earrings and tattooes and everything, but in actual fact he was very gentle and he could play beautiful guitar. They called him Snake because his cock was so long, and he really knew how to use it.

"I loved Kenneth. I really loved him. He was

easily the most handsome, clean-cut guy I'd ever been out with. But after four months I began to get restless, you know? He was great in bed, and he always satisfied me, but he was never *dangerous*. When you've been going out with somebody like Snake and some of the other boys I used to hang out with, just ordinary making love seems like, well . . . just ordinary making love.

"Perri was never quite as wild as me, but all the same she was very flirtatious. Every man she met, she made him feel that she wanted to go to bed with him, it didn't matter who it was—waiters, bank tellers, cops, the old guy behind the deli counter in the supermarket. She got on pretty good with Charles, but he worked selling insurance which meant that she hardly ever saw him in the evenings, and he was always making dates and then breaking them again, and when they *did* get together he was so tired that he wasn't very inspiring in bed.

"So I suggested a foursome. The idea was that we should all have a meal together at Kenneth's apartment, because his was the biggest, with two bedrooms. Perri and me would both act very sexy and maybe—fingers crossed!—that would loosen Kenneth up a little and give Charles some extra lead in his pencil. We didn't really plan anything, we just thought it would liven things up if we got together and fooled around. And we certainly didn't think that it would turn out the way it did!

"We had a great meal. Kenneth's a terrific cook and we had empanadas and chicken fajitas and beans and rice. We drank a lot of wine, too, and so I guess we were all very relaxed. Perri and I really laid on the flirting. I was wearing these tight pink shorts and a white T-shirt without anything underneath, so that my breasts were bouncing around all evening—oh, and pink glittery nail color, too, fingers and toes! Perri wore a sleeveless silk top, kind of a mulberry color, and the shortest skirt in the history of the world. She wasn't wearing any panties, either, but she always made sure that she sat in such a way that the guys could never quite see up her skirt. She is such a tease, I tell you.

"We played some music after dinner, but then Kenneth said, 'How about a game of Trivial Pursuit? We could play it for money . . . you know, to make it more interesting.' But I said, 'Don't let's play it for money. Let's play it for sex.' Well, we'd all had quite a few glasses of wine and a really sexy mood had built up between us. Charles was sitting on the couch and Perri was sitting on his lap; while Kenneth and me were sprawling in this big beanbag. Kenneth said, 'Sex? What do you mean, *sex*?' He was really surprised to hear something like that coming from me. Just because I'm always smart and well-dressed and nice to people, I think he'd gotten the impression that I was very demure. He hadn't wanted to try anything really wild in bed in case he shocked me, and made me think that he was some kind of a sex maniac.

"I said, 'Whoever wins can decide what all the others have to do together. You know, like a porno movie director. And they *have* to do it, no matter what it is.' It took the boys a couple of minutes to get their heads around what I was suggesting, but then Perri opened her legs a little way so that Kenneth caught a glimpse up her skirt. I knew she did it on purpose, but Kenneth didn't. All the same, it was enough to turn him on, and he said, 'Sure, okay. Sex could be more fun than money.' I think there was another deciding factor, too: Kenneth is really good at Trivial Pursuit, and he thought that he could win easy.

"Kenneth arranged the board on the floor and we all sat around. We played for a while and Kenneth and Charles were both way ahead of Perri and me and were getting a little fidgety. So Perri came up with this idea to make it even more exciting. Every time a player won a piece of pie, he or she would have to take off one piece of clothing. So if you were winning, you would end up being naked before everybody else. It was fun, but it was also a way of discouraging people from winning too quick. It didn't take long before Kenneth was down to his shorts, and I'm sure that he deliberately answered a couple of questions wrong so that he wouldn't have to take them off. I mean, even *I* know that Kirk Douglas's real name is Issur Danielovitch Demsky.

"Mind you, Perri was only wearing two pieces of clothing anyhow, and I was only wearing three, so it looked like we'd all be naked, whether we were winning or losing.

"It only took about twenty minutes before all of us were naked. It was a strange feeling, because none of us had been naked in front of another couple before. Kenneth had a huge hard-on, there was nothing he could do about it, and Perri kept winking at me and licking her lips. Charles wasn't so stiff, but his cock was lying across his thigh and it was pretty swollen, like it wouldn't take much to make it totally hard. Kenneth's dark, with a hairy chest; but Charles has very light-brown hair, and it's been bleached by the sun. He has a gorgeous body, not a spare ounce of fat anyplace at all.

"Perri's blonde, petite, with small round breasts and nipples that are almost the same color as my nails—Ridiculous Pink. You could tell that she was a natural blonde, too. She was sitting cross-legged so that her pussy was open, and her left heel was right up between her lips. I was sitting close to Kenneth. My breasts are much bigger than Perri's, in fact they're much too big for *me*, really, but I've never had a boyfriend who said he didn't like them. I kept brushing Kenneth's arm with my nipples and I think that was one reason why his cock wouldn't go down!

"Once were all naked, we all played real hard to win, even though we kept kissing and touching and there was definitely a very erotic atmosphere. I still don't know how I managed to remember the answers to half of the questions. How did I know that George Cormack invented Wheaties?

"I can't remember how long that first game took, but Kenneth won with some question about Elvis Presley. He said, 'Now I get to tell the rest of you what to do, right?' And we said, 'Right.' He said, 'Okay . . . you two girls have to fondle and cuddle each other, while Charles has to lie next to you and fondle both of you.'

"Perri said, 'Are you into lesbianism, or what?' But Kenneth said, 'The deal was *anything*, right? So I've won and that's what I want you to do.'

"We had another glass of wine, and then Perri came and sat next to me on the bean bag. She put her arm around me and kissed me, and said, 'Come on, Sally . . . let's show Kenneth how it's done. Let's make him feel really jealous.'

"I kissed her back, and then we kissed each other properly, tongues and everything. Our nipples were touching each other's breasts, and I suddenly had this huge rush of erotic feeling, you know, almost like the rush you're supposed to get with cocaine. This was really forbidden, right? Kissing another woman and caressing her breasts, and yet it was very, very sexy. Perri took one of my breasts in both of her hands and stroked my nipple with her thumbs, and at the same time she licked all along my lips with the tip of her tongue, and then poked her tongue in between my teeth.

"I took hold of both of her nipples between my fingers and gently rolled and rubbed them until they grew impossibly hard: I'd never seen nipples stick out as much as that before. I put my head down and sucked both of her nipples in turn, rolling them across the roof of my mouth with my tongue. At the same time she squeezed and fondled my breasts, and then she ran her hands all the way down my back. I shivered—you know, one of those shivers of pleasure that you simply can't stop.

"Charles came and sat down beside us. He stroked our hair, and ran his fingertips around our lips. I felt his bare leg against me, and then his cock. He was hard now—very, very hard, and he rolled his cock against my thigh with the flat of his hand, like a warm rolling pin. I couldn't resist reaching behind me and touching it, just the head of it, with the tips of my fingernails, and tickling it and scratching it a little, and then tickling and scratching his balls. I was suddenly worried what Kenneth's reaction might be, but when I looked over Perri's shoulder I saw him sitting on the floor with his back against the couch, his balls cupped in one hand and his other hand rubbing his cock. He caught my eye and gave me a smile and a shake of his head like he was saying to me, 'I love you . . . and I really can't believe you can do something like this.'

"Charles reached around me and held up my breasts so that Perri could lick and suck my nipples. It was like he was feeding her. My breasts felt extraordinary. 'Tingle' isn't the right word. 'Fizz' isn't the right word. But I guess you could call it a tingly fizz. And I feel the same sort of tingly fizz between my legs, too. I think if Perri had gone on sucking my nipples for long enough I definitely could have reached an orgasm without her even touching my cunt at all.

"But she finished sucking my breasts and she started to run her tongue down my sides and across my stomach. She poked her tongue tip into my tummy button and that was a real strange sensation, too. Then she licked even further down, right down into my pubic hair, and suddenly her tongue was actually playing with my clitoris. I had never had a woman do that to me before. I had never had a woman make love to me before. I closed my eyes and I sank my fingers into Perri's silky blond hair and I was out there, I was really out there, speeding toward the final frontier.

"Perri licked my clitoris and then I felt the tip of her tongue probing into my pee hole. It was like she was really exploring me to find out what another woman's cunt felt like in every detail, and what it tasted like. She went a little way further down, and I felt her rolled-up tongue inside my vagina. I opened my eyes and Kenneth was standing over me now, slowly jerking his cock. I reached up with one hand and took hold of it, and jerked it for him. Then I pulled him down toward me, and took his cock into my mouth, as far as it would go. I actually choked, and I had to take it out for a moment, but then I stretched my head right back and took his cock all the way into my mouth, right into my throat, so that his balls were dangling on my chin. I couldn't breathe properly, but that excited me all the more.

"At the same time, Charles went down behind me and I could feel him opening up the cheeks of my ass with his hands. His tongue slid all the way down until it reached my asshole, and he licked me around and around it, and prodded his tongue into it. Perri was still licking my cunt, and she had a tongue-fight with Charles, both of them trying to push their tongues into my vagina at the same time. Kenneth kept on fucking my mouth, taking his cock right out and then sliding it all the way back in again. His whole body was tense, his legs were tense, and he was holding on to the table for support.

"Charles and Perri started finger-fucking me, in competition with each other. Perri slid a finger into my vagina so Charles slid in two. So Perri pushed in three—at least, that's what it felt like. So Charles pushed a finger into my asshole, and Perri followed with two. Their fingers wriggled inside me, touching each other, playing with each other. They were flirting and teasing each other, but they were doing it inside me, right up inside my vagina, right up inside my ass.

"After a while Charles took his fingers out and raised himself up behind me. He positioned his cock between my legs, with the head of it nestling between the lips of my cunt. He didn't push it up me right away. He let Perri lick it, and lick my lips all around it, and then at last he sank it into me. He started to fuck me, while Perri kept on licking my clitoris and sucking his balls. I was so wet with juice and saliva between my legs that I felt as if I was flooded.

"Charles kissed my neck and my ears from behind. Kenneth took his cock out of my mouth and Charles stretched over my shoulder and kissed my cheek. Then, when Kenneth leaned forward again, Charles took hold of Kenneth's cock and sucked it himself. I had never seen a man sucking another man's cock before, not even in videos. I was shocked . . . but then I was on a tremendous sexual high, and everything seemed possible, and everything seemed permissible. I licked all around Charles's lips while he sucked Kenneth's cock, and I licked Kenneth's cock, too, and nuzzled his balls. Kenneth took his cock out of Charles's mouth and plunged it back into mine; and then back into Charles's, one after the other.

Then he started to come; he was too excited to stop himself. It came pumping out of him like he was never going to stop. He covered our faces in sperm, and used his cock to rub it all over our lips and our cheeks and our foreheads and our chins. I licked all the sperm from Charles's face and he licked all the sperm from mine.

"Charles started to fuck me faster. Perri's tongue was still flicking my clitoris and I knew that I wouldn't be able to stop myself from coming, either. Charles suddenly climaxed, right up inside me, and I started to climax, too. I didn't want Perri to stop licking me but at the same time I felt that I would die if she didn't. I had such an orgasm that I was flinging my arms and my legs around.

"There was a moment when we all rolled away from each other and lay on the floor gasping. But it didn't stop there. I was still too aroused, still too excited, and Perri was too. We had another glass of wine, all panting, all looking at each other as if something incredible had happened, which it had. Then I gently pushed Perri back onto the bean bag. She didn't resist. She just smiled. I opened up her legs and right in front of everybody I started to lick her blonde-haired cunt. I thought that if *she* could do it, then I could, too. There was her clitoris sticking out, and the tip of my tongue only just touching it. There were my lips, sucking in a mouthful of plump flesh and pubic hair. She had such a subtle taste, like nothing I'd ever tasted before. I can't describe it. I just knew that it was nectar and I wanted more of it.

"Kenneth and Charles were both watching us and playing with their cocks. It only took Charles about ten minutes before his cock came up again, and Kenneth's soon followed. They sat close to each other, rubbing the heads of their cocks together and feeling each other's balls. Then while I was still licking Perri, I saw Charles rolling a condom onto Kenneth's cock, and then I saw Charles going down on his hands and knees, lifting his butt as high as he could. I thought: *My God, what are they doing?* Kenneth said, 'Hold on a moment, sweetheart.' I raised my head and he reached over and put his hand between Perri's thighs, digging his fingers deep into her cunt, really squeezing it, really massaging it. Perri moaned and shifted her hips on the bean bag. But Kenneth took his hand away and smeared her juices between the cheeks of Charles's ass. Then he knelt behind him, gripping his cock in his hand, and both Perri and me watched him with our mouths open as he forced his cock into Charles's asshole. Charles was gritting his teeth as Kenneth's cock went deeper and deeper, but he didn't cry out or anything, and his own cock was rearing up hard. Kenneth slowly managed to pull himself forward until his cock had completely disappeared into Charles's ass.

"Kenneth fucked Charles a few times, and then

he eased himself over sideways, with his cock still deep inside him. He lay on his back with Charles sitting on top of him, and Charles slowly eased himself up and down. When he lifted himself up, I could see his asshole tight around Kenneth's cock. When he went down, their balls touched, and I couldn't resist bending my head forward and taking a bite at all four of them.

"Perri sat up and said, 'This isn't fair . . . I'm the only one who hasn't been fucked.' I said, 'Well, go on then, now's your chance. Charles's cock is going begging.' She stood astride Charles, facing him. She opened her cunt with her fingers and slowly rotated her hips, rubbing herself against his face. Then she gradually hunkered down, reaching down with her left hand and taking hold of Charles's cock. I stood behind her to help her sit on it. She threw back her head and said, 'Aaaah, that's so good.'

"She's very fit, and she was able to ride up and down on Charles's cock like she was doing some really elegant gym exercise. She was holding on to his shoulders, but only lightly, and her stomach was kind of undulating every time she went up and down. Her thighs were wide apart, and I could see his cock actually sliding inside her, and out again, and it looked as if her cunt was actually trying to suck at it. At the same time, Kenneth was pushing his cock deep into Charles's ass—not in and out, he couldn't do that with Charles's weight on him, but by thrusting his hips upward.

"Charles came first. It didn't surprise me, with Kenneth's cock up his ass and Perri dancing on *his* cock.

"Perri stood up, with a long string of sperm dangling out of her cunt. Charles lifted himself off Kenneth's cock, which was still hard, and Kenneth pulled off his condom. Perri lay back on the bean bag and Kenneth climbed on top of her. He gave her a hard, urgent fuck, while Charles and I sat close behind them, egging them on with all kinds of dirty language. Perri was red in the face and absolutely covered in sweat. Her nipples were standing up and there was a flush across her chest. I could see her thighs tensing and her hands gripping Kenneth's hips. She suddenly squeezed her face tight and climaxed, and Kenneth climaxed, too.

"I can't honestly remember how long we all lay there afterward. We finished the wine, the candles burned down. We took turns showering and then we all went to bed. I didn't say anything much to Kenneth that night. I had watched him fuck another woman and he had watched me fuck another man. Not only that, he had fucked Charles, too, and I had gone down on Perri. My feelings were very, very complicated.

"In the morning we couldn't pretend that nothing had happened. I was worried that everybody was going to be embarrassed and remote, but we weren't. We kissed each other and held each other, and I think we all recognized that what we had done was maybe a once-in-a-lifetime experience, but we had done it out of friendship and love, and we had all learned something about ourselves and each other—something that we never would have known if we hadn't played that game of Trivial Pursuit."

In the case of Sally and her friends, a board game became the license for the foursome to act without any sexual inhibition whatever. All four of them had strong suppressed urges, but the game gave them "permission" to bring them out into the open and act them out for real. This is what I meant by sexual play having to have rules. If you abide by the rules, then you don't feel that you're personally responsible for what's happening, even if you invented the rules yourself. The rules restrict what you do, but they also give you the freedom to do what you want.

None of the players in this game of Trivial Pursuit thought of themselves as homosexuals. They enjoyed their sexual experimentation with a member of the same sex, but as Sally later remarked, "None of us were going to make a career out of it." Kenneth said to her that he had always wondered what it would be like to make love to another man, and now that he had tried it, his curiosity was completely satisfied, and he didn't feel the need to do it again. "Too much like hard work."

Sally admitted that she still occasionally had fantasies about making love to Perri, but she recognized them for what they were—fantasies. She thought about Perri sometimes when she was making love to Kenneth, "and they really help to turn me on." Her lovemaking with Kenneth since they all played Trivial Pursuit was "much, much closer, much more experimental, freer, wilder . . . even wilder than it used to be with Snake."

Almost any game can be adapted to include an element of erotica, and almost any game can be a catalyst for a more exciting sex life. You don't have to have a foursome, of course; there are countless games that two can play.

The best game of all, though, is afterward, when the cards have been shuffled and the dice have been rolled, and you're in bed together.

Now we've taken a look at sexy games, let's take a look at sexy toys.

8

The Wayward Buzz

When vibrators were first advertised in the 1960s, they were discreetly described as "soothing aid for hypertension, tired muscles, and rheumatism." They were illustrated by photographs of sweetly smiling girls applying their vibrators to their aching shoulders, and not a word was said about the obvious application of a phallic-shaped object that happened to give you a pleasant buzz when you switched it on.

As time went by and publishing strictures relaxed, the advertising became much less coy, although it still wasn't openly admitted that vibrators might be used for masturbation. Vibrators themselves, which had started life as smooth, featureless cylinders, were supplied with slip-on latex sleeves to give them more than a passing resemblance to an erect male organ. By the early 1970s they were actually being molded in the shape of real penises, and even better-than-real penises.

These days, sex toy advertisements make no bones about what they're selling and what they're used for. We're no longer embarrassed about self-stimulation, and there are hundreds of different devices that are specifically designed to give us the maximum enjoyment when we masturbate.

You can still buy a garden variety 7-inch vibrator for about 15 dollars, but there's no mention of rheumatism in its advertisement. "Take a good look at this superlative pussy-pleaser—firm penis head, thick-veined shaft texture like flesh, and variable-speed vibrations." For 20 dollars, you can have the 9-inch version, which is twice as thick.

Some vibrators are said to be modeled after the penises of real porno stars, such as the black sex actor Sean Michael. "Feel the pleasure of Sean's flesh!" the advertisement exclaims. "Renowned for his ample equipment, Sean Michael's dong can now be yours for your own personal excitement! Made in unique fleshy latex and sculpted from his actual penis, this black masterpiece is guaranteed to make him or her gulp! Over 10 inches in length and detailed with every vein and wrinkle, this sensational super-dong can now be yours!"

It's interesting that the advertisement unashamedly suggests that Mr. Michael's equipment might be equally attractive to a man. Almost all vibrators and anal probes these days carry the recommendation that they are "suitable for both men and women," and the stigma of "lonely loser" that used to be attached to men and women who have to seek sexual satisfaction on their own has almost completely evaporated.

A device called the Techno-Flex, a "new-generation vibrator," is completely sexless in appearance, but it obviously has no purpose other than stimulating the vagina or the anus. It is pearl-blue, with a 4-inch vibrating head on the end of a 12-inch flexible shaft. Its makers claim that "it enables the user to go as deep and at any angle so desired."

Apart from those sexual devices that can be used by both sexes, there are many new stimulators that are designed specifically for women. The classic is Joni's Butterfly, a variable-speed vibrating pad that you fasten over your vulva with straps so that it remains in position while you gradually buzz yourself to an orgasm. New on the market is the Inflatable Mouse, which is a little pink plastic vibrator, no more than 4½ inches long, with three thick nubs on one side. It starts off small, but once you've inserted it, you can inflate it with a hand-squeezed bulb so that it becomes bigger and bigger and, in the words of the catalog, "will soon fill your passionate love-chasm."

There are several jelly-soft vibrators and dildoes that have the feel and consistency of a half-hard erection. The most popular of these is Mr. Softee. "The delicious feel of a real penis . . . see it, squeeze it, touch it!" It may *feel* real, but it is produced in an alarming shade of cerise, and other jelly vibrators come in bright blue and poisonous green. Probably the most complicated is the Mega-Man, which not only vibrates but has an internal rotating motion at the same time, so that it appears to squirm. Mega-Man has a rippled shaft and a small probe attached to the base at 45 degrees with tiny springy antennae on it. This can be used either for clitoral or anal stimulation, so that you can squirm and tickle at the same time.

Love balls, which were first used by concubines in ancient China to keep themselves in a state of constant sexual arousal, are still available today, although they're usually gold-painted plastic rather than hand-carved ivory. Four shiny balls about 1½ inches in diameter are attached to a foot-long cord and inserted one by one into your vagina. Each ball contains a weight, so that as you move they all gyrate and wobble, which (for some women) produces a highly pleasurable sensation. You can keep them in all day, if you wish, and the same goes for Vibro-panties, which are a tight-fitting pair of panties with a latex vibrating dildo in the crotch. The advertisement for Vibro-panties shows a woman standing in line at a supermarket checkout with a dreamy expression on her face.

You can buy a whole variety of panties containing vibrators or built-in dildoes, mostly in PVC or latex. Sadie, 25, a photographer's model from Los Angeles, California, said that she acquired a pair from a specialist rubberwear company after she had posed for a series of fashion pictures in rubber skirts and dresses. "The guy was showing us his catalog, and when I saw these panties I said, for a joke, 'Oh *yes*, I must have a pair of these!' They have a big dildo built into the front of them and a thinner dildo built into the back, so that they excite you in two holes at the same time. The guy said, sure, and give me a pair, even though my friends and I were screaming with laughter. I took them home but I never seriously thought about wearing them for real. I just used to show them to people just for laughs.

"But then I found a new boyfriend, Josh. He's twenty-seven and he runs his own print shop. He's very handsome, dark hair, designer stubble, but very quiet. We met when I took in some of my pictures to be printed up. He asked me out a couple of times and I really liked him. He was terrific looking but he wasn't at all vain, you know, like so many good-looking guys. He wasn't very pushy, either, which I liked in a way, but on the other hand I wouldn't have minded at all if he had tried to make a move on me. So after the second date I invited him back to my place for a glass of wine, and played some smoochy music and we started kissing and everything.

"But then he said, 'Listen, I can't do this, I have a girlfriend already.' I said, 'what does that matter? You're not *engaged*, are you?' He said no, but everybody expected him to marry her. They used to be high school sweethearts and their families both assumed that they were going to stay together for the rest of their lives. The trouble was, he wasn't sure that he really loved her any more—you know, sexually.

"I said, 'If you're not sure, don't do it.' But he said he felt committed. I asked him if she was as sexy as me. He didn't want to answer that. So I picked up those rubber panties and said, 'I bet she doesn't have underwear like this!' I'll tell you, his mouth dropped open. Then I told him where I had got them from, and we laughed about them, but after a while he said, 'No . . . I can't see Clarisse wearing anything like that,' and even though he was laughing there was kind of a serious tone in his voice.

"I didn't see Josh for a few days and then I had to go down to have some more copies of my model card printed. He came over and said hi and apologized because he hadn't been in touch, but he had to spend some time helping Clarisse's parents, who were moving into a new apartment. I asked him how he was, and how Clarisse was, and he said fine. He asked me out for a pizza after work and I ummed and aahed and then I said, 'Okay.' Then . . . just while he was opening the door for me, I said, 'You remember those panties I showed you?' He said, 'Sure . . . who could forget them?' I said, 'I'll let you into a secret. I'm wearing them now, and I'm going to be wearing them tonight.'

"He didn't say a word, but you should have seen the color of his face. As a matter of fact, I *wasn't* wearing them, but I thought if this was going to be a fight between me and Clarisse, then I'd better use the one weapon that I knew would give me an edge, and that was sex.

"I went home and had a shower and washed my hair. Come on, I was going to be a real fox this evening. I gave my cunt a fresh shave, and I smothered myself all over with body lotion. Then I took those rubber panties and massaged KY jelly into the dildoes so that they were good and slippery. I stepped into them and tugged them up. They were very, very tight . . . so tight that I had to sprinkle some talcum powder onto my thighs to ease them up higher. They made a rubbery squeaking noise and they smelled so rubbery, too.

"I positioned the front dildo in my cunt and then I reached behind me and positioned the rear dildo up against my asshole. I wriggled the panties up a little bit more, but my asshole was rebelling against the rear dildo and it was real hard to get it inside. So in the end I turned around and slowly sat down on the end of the bed, so that the dildo was forced right up my ass by my own weight. It had ridges on it, and it was a little cold, and I could feel it go in every inch of the way. But once it was in, it was in. The front dildo was halfway up my cunt, so I gave the panties a last few pulls and I was filled right up.

"Looking at those panties, you never could have told that I had two rubber cocks up inside me. They were just so tight. I put on my little blue sleeveless dress. I'd been thinking about wearing my white one but of course my panties were black rubber and they showed right through.

"At first the muscles in my asshole kept flinching because I'd never had anything up there before, except for one boyfriend's finger, a couple of times. But it's surprising how quickly you can get used to it, and begin to enjoy it. It was like being kept open all the time, waiting for a man to take you; and the dildo in my cunt was bliss. It had a big knobbly head on it, and I could feel it virtually fucking me every time I walked around. When I sat down, I had to sit down real careful because it went in so deep.

"The sexiest thing to do when wearing those panties was to sit right on the edge of your chair and move your butt up and down a little, not so that anybody could notice you doing it, and squeeze your pelvic floor muscles at the same time, the way they tell you in exercise class. I tried it that afternoon, while I was sitting in the studio, going through a whole stack of pictures. At first I didn't think it was having any effect, but then I suddenly realized that I was growing tenser and tenser, and that the knobbly head of that front dildo was rubbing inside my cunt, and that back dildo was making my asshole feel as if it had been stung by bees. The photographer's secretary was sitting only three or four feet away from me, and she didn't realize how close I was to having an orgasm. I was pushing my elbows down on the desk in front of me, and I was bobbing my butt up and down, quicker and quicker. I felt incredibly hot, in spite of the air-conditioning, and I knew that my cheeks were flushed. Then I clenched my thighs together and I came. My muscles wanted to force those two dildoes out of me, but of course they were held in tight, and so I kept on coming and coming and I thought I was never going to be able to stop. I cried out loud and I had to pretend that I was having a coughing fit.

"The secretary gave me a funny look but of course she had no way of knowing that I had been quietly fucking myself for the past twenty minutes.

"Josh picked me up outside the studio. We went for a drink and we talked and we laughed, but in the end he just had to ask me. He said, 'Are you really wearing those panties or were you just putting me on?' I kissed him and said, 'Do you want to find out?'

"He looked at me for a long time and he knew I was playing a game. I was, I admit it. I don't normally wear fetish underwear and go around all day with two dildoes stuck up inside me. But I was playing the part of a seductive vamp, and that was the costume that went along with the part. I wanted Josh, I admit it, and if that was what it took to get him, then so be it.

"We left the cocktail bar and Josh drove me home. I remember that there was Tina Turner playing on the car stereo—"What's Love Got to Do With It." I don't think we said more than a couple of words to each other the whole way back. We didn't need to. We were like two people in a movie, following the script. If you're not certain how make a success of your life, if you don't know how to get what you want, you should try it some time. Just play the part of you, being successful; or you, getting what you want.

"Back at my apartment, Josh and I were kissing and caressing each other even before we managed to close the front door. It was like we were on fire. I unbuttoned Josh's shirt and unbuckled his belt, and he pulled down the zipper on my dress and it dropped right down to the floor. He looked at my tight black rubber panties and said, 'I can't believe it . . . you're actually wearing them.' I said, 'Yes, and you have no idea how much they turn me on. I've been thinking about you all day while I've been wearing these, and do you know something . . ." I opened his pants and reached into his boxer shorts. His dick was sticking out as hard as rock. I gripped it in my hand as I knelt down to pull off his pants and shorts, and I couldn't resist giving it a lick at the same time. It had that animal taste that always turns me on. If they could bottle that, they'd have the greatest sex-potion of all time.

"I stood up again and Josh kissed me and took off my bra. He touched my breasts, and he has this very erotic way of cupping my breasts in his fingers, very lightly, and then gradually drawing them together toward my nipples, until he gives each nipple a gentle rub between his fingers and thumb, and it's sensational.

"We went over to the couch. It's huge, this couch, with big cream linen cushions. I lay down on it and Josh sat next to me, kissing me, kissing my nipples, running his fingers all the way down me until I felt so sexy and sensitive that I didn't think I was going to be able to bear it any longer.

"He ran his hands over my panties, touching me between my legs, and then he began to roll my panties down. They were so tight that he had to pull them really hard, and of course my skin was all sweaty underneath. But at last he managed to get them down to my hips, so that he could see the big black rubber dildo sliding out of my cunt, and the thin dildo sliding out of my asshole. My cunt was so wet that the dildo made a sucking noise when it came out.

"He pulled my panties right off, and then he climbed on top of me. He didn't have to ask me if my cunt was ready for him. It was wide open and warm and very, very juicy. He eased his dick into me and I lifted my hips and looked down so that I could watch it disappear inside me. 'That's like a magic trick,' I told him. 'The disappearing dick.' He said, 'If anybody's worked any magic around here, it's you. You've given me a reason for breaking up with Clarisse.'

"I didn't lie to him. I didn't say that I was sorry, or that I hadn't meant it to happen. I lay back and I looked up into his handsome face and felt his dick right up inside me, and I loved it, I loved every second of it. I closed my eyes, and he could sense that I wasn't in any hurry because he fucked me real slow, while I ran my fingers all the way down his back and gripped the cheeks of his ass.

"He whispered, 'Tell me what it's like, with that dildo up your cunt all day.' And I said, 'Gorgeous, but nothing like as gorgeous as you. I don't need a dildo anymore. I want you up my cunt all day. And all night, too.' He fucked me faster and faster, and when he climaxed he literally shouted out loud.

"I've only worn those panties once since Josh and I got together. That was when he had to take

a trip to New York for six days. But the third day
I was missing him so much that I put them on and
called him at his hotel. I told him that I was wearing them and that they reminded me so much of
him that I was turning myself on. I said he ought
to masturbate while I was talking to him, because
then he'd have an idea of how excited I was feeling, with those two rubber dildoes up inside me. I
said he ought to stroke and pull his cock and
imagine it was me who was doing it. I said I was
going to wear those panties until he got home
and then I was going to let him take them off and
fuck me, but only after he'd sucked both dildoes
for me.

"I went on and on, talking so dirty that I was
getting excited myself. In the end, I heard Josh say,
'Ohhh . . . that's it, you've done it. I've just shot
out, all over my stomach.'

"I got pretty good value out of those panties,
didn't I? Especially since I didn't even have to pay
for them."

Erotic underwear and sex toys can liven up
your love life dramatically, but only if you use it,
as Sadie did, as a way of showing how you feel.
Underwear on its own is not going to seduce the
man of your wildest sexual dreams, *you* are. You
won't be able to guess the number of complaints
I've received from women who have bought sexy
underwear and sex aids to arouse their partners,
only to find that "they didn't do any good." That's

because it's not the clothes or the toys themselves that strike the sexual spark, it's the person who's wearing them or the person who's using them. Think what kind of a woman will excite the man you want, and then dress accordingly. You don't need to spend a lot of money, or even spend any money at all.

Jinnie, a 22-year-old hairdresser, said that her boyfriend couldn't resist her in soaking-wet white cotton panties, just plain ones, so she always wore them in the yard when she was watering her vegetables. And talking of vegetables, Ricki, a 29-year-old doctor's receptionist, said that she could always excite her husband by openly masturbating with a large cucumber.

The versatility of modern-day materials has meant that sex toys have wildly increased in variety. You can now buy clear plexiglass vibrators that light up inside your vagina; or vibrators that glow in the dark. Some products are now being produced in a new latex called Cyberskin, which is formulated to feel even more like natural flesh. For women, there's the Natural Cyberskin Dong With Balls, "a profound, majestic, 8-inch replica with all the natural qualities you can think of . . . with an erection that has the lifelike stiffness but fleshy softness of an actual penis . . . plus soft squeezable balls, realistic glans and veins, all detailed to perfection."

You can also buy a Natural Cyberskin Extension, which is a latex sleeve that slides onto your partner's penis but gives him 2 inches of added length. The advertisers say that it feels comfortable and "more importantly, she won't know the difference," which is a claim I tend to dispute. If your lover's penis suddenly turned out to be two inches longer, I suspect that you would notice it. You might not complain about it, but you would notice it.

Men are very well catered to these days when it comes to masturbatory sex aids. The possible advantage of these from a woman's point of view is that they can help to restore a man's erection if he has been going through a period of impotence or if he has been unable to achieve and maintain a really hard penis during lovemaking.

I have covered the subject of impotence quite thoroughly in previous books. It has almost as many different causes as it has sufferers, and overcoming it has to be dealt with in a very caring and individual way.

Almost all men experience a falling-away of libido and sexual prowess as they pass their fiftieth year. This is simply a consequence of age, although it can be ameliorated by good diet, regular exercise, and—most important of all—a positive attitude toward life. Depression and chronic pessimism are very real conditions, and they can have a devastating effect on a man's sexual abilities.

Alcohol also impairs a man's performance in bed, especially if he has been drinking heavily over a long period fo time. It can start with occasional failures to perform, and then, as time goes by, become almost complete impotence. Some drugs have side effects that can cause complete or partial impotence, and so can many medical problems such as diabetes. Whatever the apparent cause of impotence, it's worth your partner talking to his doctor. There are several ways in which clinical impotence can be cured, from a course of testosterone to Viagra tablets.

I have talked to a considerable number of men who have taken Viagra to tackle their impotence, and the success rate seems to be hearteningly high. I must emphasize, though, that your partner should not take Viagra until his doctor has checked his general fitness; and that no man should take Viagra unless he genuinely needs it. It will not radically improve the sexual performance of a man who can already perform perfectly well, and there may be risks of long-term physical side effects.

If your partner is suffering from no more than the drooping effects of tiredness or stress or a lack of sexual self-confidence, there is a lot you can do to help. Don't ever feel that your lover is failing to get an erection because he no longer finds you sexually attractive (or, if you do feel it, which is understandable, try not to show it.) Continue to be loving and sexy and attentive, even when he can't get it up. At that moment when he's tried to enter you and failed, he'll be feeling at his blackest and his angriest, and it's critical that you show him that you still find him virile.

Don't turn your back on him. I know that you may be feeling angry and disappointed, too. But if you reject him you will make him feel much worse and it will make it much more difficult for him to overcome his impotence—for which *you* will suffer, too.

Don't say that you really don't mind. He's not stupid. Of course you mind, as much as he minds. He doesn't want to be talked to like a child who's dropped his jelly in his lap. He needs more than anything else to feel like a man.

Don't make a strenuous attempt to rub him into an erection. He'll be too self-conscious about his failure to achieve one spontaneously, and even if you do manage to stiffen him up for a while, he will be feeling desperately anxious that it won't last, and sure enough, as soon as he starts worrying about it, down it will sink—making him feel even more inadequate than he did to begin with.

Take hold of his softened penis and affectionately squish it. That's important. That shows that you still like touching it, even if it's temporarily let you down. Then take hold of your partner's hand and guide it between your legs, and show him that he can still satisfy you with his fingers and his

tongue. Lie back and encourage him to masturbate you and/or give you cunnilingus. If you
show him how much pleasure he's giving you,
there's a possibility that his penis may arise as
you become more and more excited, and that he
will be able to penetrate you. Only a possibility,
mind. If you feel his penis bob up against you, you
can loosely hold it and give it an occasional rub,
but don't give your lover the impression that
you're desperately trying to jerk it into full hardness. If it softens again, keep on holding it for
a while, keep on gently fondling it. Your lover
will be extremely over-sensitive about his lack of
sexual performance, and if you let go of his penis
as soon as it begins to subside he could well take
that to mean "oh, well, then, if it's not going to
stand up, I can't be bothered with it." Irrational, of
course, but we're talking about a man who has
been unable to give you proof of his manhood.

If his failure to achieve an erection persists for
any length of time, and there is no obvious medical problem, then it is worthwhile to try some of
the male masturbatory sex aids that are on the
market today. You can use any one of them to help
him achieve an erection before making love. Then,
if necessary, you can use a restrictive strap or brace
to maintain it.

What is really important is to build up his
sexual confidence again—to introduce a new routine in which he can achieve an erection and keep

it up long enough to make love to you. You will probably find that you don't need to do it more than two or three times before his penis hardens naturally, and you can put the sex aid back in its box.

The simplest sex aid is sold under a variety of different names, such as Silklips. It's a latex sleeve that fits over the penis. It's connected to a hand-operated pump that you rhythmically squeeze in order to create a sucking sensation. "Silklips slides up and down your penis like a loving pair of moist wet lips ... it's so incredibly satisfying, you'll think it's her!"

A more 21st-century masturbatory aid is the Super Thruster, also known as the New Jel-Lee Cock Stroker. Molded out of clear blue jelly plastic, this is a sleeve filled with soft projecting fingers into which your partner can thrust his lubricated penis. It looks rather like a large hair-roller with the bobbles on the inside instead of the outside. The Super Thruster is connected to a vibrator mechanism that is intended to "massage your flesh to a frenzy!" Its "unique transparent jelly material allows you to watch"—so that as an interested party, you can see for yourself when your lover is ready for action.

Another device is the so-called penis developer, which was invented in the 1960s by my old friend, the late Dr. Robert Chartham. A deluxe version is called Handsome Up. This is essentially a transparent tube, like a large test tube, in which your lover's penis can be inserted through an airtight cuff. You then evacuate air from the test-tube with a hand- or power-pump, and your lover's penis swells to fill the vacuum. You can see how big it's growing because the tube is calibrated in inches and centimeters.

Regular use of the penis developer is supposed to enlarge a man's penis but there is no evidence that it has any dramatic or lasting effect. However, it is quite a spectacular way of giving your lover an erection.

If the penis developer seems too technical, there are dozens of male masturbators that simulate the female vagina. That's if you don't mind competition from—say—a Pamela Anderson look-alike vagina. "This luscious pussy has all the necessary refinements to make it unbelievably lifelike . . . just part her vaginal lips, push yourself in and feel the instant sensations of her lusthole." Pamela's Pussy comes complete with pubic hair.

Then there's Pussy-Orgasmus—"detailed to perfection with protruding clitoris and soft supple labia . . . with variable power vibrations and inflatable sleeve for lifelike gripping." The Doc Johnson Incredibly Realistic Vagina is claimed to be "hand-molded from an actual vagina." It has pubic hair, real-feel vaginal lips and adjustable vibro-power, which is something that real vaginas unfortunately lack.

If your partner's tastes run to something tighter, there's the new Anal Amazon, another creation in jelly latex that is supposed to feel like "a nice tight ass."

Once your lover has achieved an erection, your number one priority is to make sure that he doesn't lose it. There are scores of different devices for doing this, but essentially they all have the same function: to prevent the blood that has swollen the penis from flowing back into the body again.

I talked to a professional male stripper who confessed that before every show he took copies of *Hustler* to the men's room and masturbated. When his penis was erect, he tied a thin piece of nylon stocking around it to stop it from shrinking. "The women in the audience always ask me why their husbands are never hung like me."

I don't recommend a piece of stocking. You could easily tie it too tight and find it almost impossible to remove. You try the De Luxe Erection Ring, which is a simple vinyl ring with six bands around it, designed to slip over the base of the penis when soft so that it will cinch it tightly when hard. Then there's the Menfit Erection Strengthener, which looks (and works) rather like a bolo necktie, so that you can adjust it for tightness. The Superflex Grip is a latex ring filled with silicone liquid to make it extra stretchy, and a pressure-pad "to excite and further grip the urethra." The

Virility Cock Ring is also filled with silicone but it has a pearl-effect pressure pad that looks "expensively erotic," whatever that is.

Simple as they are, any one of these aids can be of considerable help to your partner in maintaining his erection once he's managed to get one, and they can certainly help to restore his sexual confidence. It's important when he's using a masturbating device to get an erection that you join in. Don't just lie there watching him while he inserts his penis into whatever gizmo you've decided to buy. *You* operate the pump. *You* control the vibrator. Ask him whether it's buzzing fast enough for him, or whether it's gripping him tightly enough. This may essentially be a sexual therapy session, but you can make it into a lighthearted sexual game that you're playing together. The friskier you are, the more fun you are, the sexier you are, the easier your partner will find it to regain his virility.

Sue-Ann, a 36-year-old homemaker from Memphis, Tennessee, said that her husband, Kyle, a broker, had been under "horrific" pressure at work, and that his sexual performance had "just died away."

"He used to be such a stud. He made love to me four, five times a week. It was very rare for us to go to bed and not have sex. Sometimes I used to wish that he wasn't quite so passionate, but I surely changed my mind about that when he started having problems. It happened once, after a company dinner, and neither of us thought anything about it, because Kyle had been drinking pretty heavy that evening. But then the same thing happened again the following week, and then again, and after only six or seven weeks he was scarcely able to get it up at all.

"The first thing that went through my mind was that he was having an affair. I guess all women think that, when their husbands pay them less and less attention in bed. I knew that he had employed a new personal assistant two or three months before, a woman called Julie, and I began to think that it might be her, because he kept talking about her all the time, what a help she was, how wonderful she was.

"I paid a visit to the office, unannounced, to check her out. Before I went in to see Kyle I spent some time chatting to this charming middle-aged black woman. She told me all about her kids and her husband and how she was coming up to her silver wedding anniversary. I asked her if she knew Kyle's new personal assistant, Julie, and if she was very sexy. She said, 'She sure is. She's a maneater. She's me.'

"It was then that I began to realize that there was something actually wrong with Kyle himself. I knew that he was under a whole lot of stress, and I knew that he'd been drinking more than was good for him, but it had never occurred to me before that it might affect his performance in the sack. So that evening I sat down and I talked to him about it. I told him that I loved him and that he was the sexist man alive, but he was having a problem and we needed to do something about it before it got any worse.

"He was so relieved that I wanted to discuss it and that I wanted to help him to get over it. He was brought up to think that a man has to be able to do everything: take care of his family, make a pile of money, drink everybody else under the table, beat all his friends at golf, and then go home and make love to his wife like King Kong. But these days, the pressures are too much. Something has got to give, and in Kyle's case his cock started waving the white flag.

"Well, we changed all that. Kyle went to the doctor for a physical, and the doctor told him to quit drinking for a while. I think it was important that the doctor told him that, rather than me, because he wouldn't have taken any notice of me. But when the doctor says that you're doing your liver some serious damage and you're shrinking your balls and you're affecting your virility . . . well, Kyle sat up and took notice.

"Then we took up tai chi together, every Tuesday evening. Over the past two or three years, we had almost stopped going out together on weekday evenings because of the pressure of Kyle's work, but we had a shared goal in overcoming Kyle's sexual problem and so we both put that one evening aside for tai chi and it was absolutely sacrosanct. We did it at home, too, early in the morning as often as we could, and after only two or three weeks I began to notice that Kyle was visibly more relaxed and more like his old self. You know, I'd almost forgotten what he used to be like before. That's how stress can creep up on you.

"After a while he was able to get erections again, but when he tried to make love to me they went down again. He began to get all frustrated and panicky again, so I decided to go along with your recommendation and try a sex aid to see if I couldn't get Kyle back into the habit of getting really hard erections and keeping them.

"I ordered one of those transparent masturbating sleeves, and a penis ring. I told Kyle what I was going to do, and I tried to be positive about it, and give him the impression that I was dying to play with it. The truth was that I *was* dying to play with it, especially if it worked!

"When it arrived I called Kyle at the office and told him, and I said 'you and I are going to have some real fun tonight.' I thought that was a good idea: giving him the whole day to think about it. When he arrived home, I didn't have a candlelit dinner waiting or anything like that. I didn't want him to feel that this was too much of a special occasion, and that if it didn't work, he'd be letting me down.

"All the same, I showed him the package as soon as he came through the door. We opened it up together and I have to say I was a little disappointed because it didn't look very sexy. Just a blue tube with a vibrator attached to it. But I said, 'Come on, let's try it.'

"Kyle wanted a shower so we took one together and I soaped him all over and rubbed his cock for him and fondled his balls. His cock started to rise when I did that, and I knelt down in front of him in the shower and sucked it for a while, until it was really hard. It was still hard when we got out of the shower and dried each other, and I guess that Kyle was probably capable of making love to me right then and there, but I didn't want to risk another disappointment.

"Sure enough, his cock began to sink, and by the time we were back in the bedroom it was soft again. But we sat on the bed and I squeezed out a big dollop of the lubricant that was supplied with the masturbator, and smothered Kyle's cock with it. I fitted the cock ring around the base of his cock. Then I pushed it into the sleeve, giving it a good squeeze with my hand. I said, 'How does that feel? Good?' and he nodded. I switched on the vibrator and it made a soft buzzing sound. I couldn't imagine what it feel like, but inside the sleeve I could see that Kyle's cock was growing bigger and harder.

"Kyle said, 'I feel kind of stupid doing this,' but I said, 'No, you don't. You and I, we're going to enjoy ourselves . . . that's what we married each other for.' And then I sprang my surprise. I brought out a jelly dildo that I'd bought for myself. It's great. It's a full-sized man's cock, complete with balls, made out of this really soft rubbery stuff. And it's shocking pink! It's exactly like a cock that isn't fully stiff, and even though I didn't say so, I wanted to show Kyle that even a pretty soft cock can still give a woman a really good time.

"I loosened my bathrobe and opened my legs. I sat up close to Kyle so that he could see everything. I pushed the dildo into my cunt and said, 'There. Now I can get turned on, too.' I don't think Kyle knew what to say, so I took his hand and guided it between my legs so that he could push the dildo in and out of me. I stretched my cunt lips wide apart and said, 'Come on, Kyle, you're amazing.'

"That dildo was amazing. It felt exactly like a cock that's just started to go limp, but has still got enough stiffness in it to go up your cunt. I started to get very turned on, and Kyle could see that I was, because I was brimming with juice. He took his cock out of the masturbator and it was bigger and stiffer than I had ever seen it before. He climbed on top of me and kissed me, and held my breasts in his hands, and then he slowly plunged that enormous cock right into me. I think that was one of the great moments of our marriage.

"He fucked me for almost twenty minutes, and his cock stayed totally hard. The feeling was absolutely sensational—and it wasn't just the physical feeling. It was the feeling of relief that everything was going to be all right again, and that Kyle and I had gotten our sex life back. It was so rejuvenating, so restoring. We came together, or almost together, and then we held each other very, very close. I felt like repeating my marriage vows all over again, except that I think they ought to say 'for richer, for poorer, for harder, for softer.' "

Sue-Ann used lightheartedness and sexual play to solve a very serious dysfunction which, unchecked, could have badly affected or even ended her marriage. I hear so many stories of relationships that have broken up over sexual difficulties, even though most of those difficulties were caused by comparatively trivial problems. For every man who finds it difficult to make love to his partner because he has started an affair with somebody new, or because he no longer found her sexually attractive, there are dozens who are suffering from nothing more than stress, money worries, fatigue, unbalanced diet, or over-indulgence in alcohol or drugs.

Sue-Ann cleverly bought a sex toy for herself so

that Kyle was more inclined to feel that they were simply playing erotic games together.

"Kyle doesn't need the masturbator now. He gets an erection naturally, and keeps it up naturally, and our sex life is better than it was when we first met. We still have a few sex toys, though. I have a weakness for that jelly-soft dildo, and sometimes Kyle uses it on me as part of his foreplay, and sometimes—when Kyle is away on business trips—I use it on myself.

"My advice to anybody whose sex life is flagging would be to think about buying one or two sex toys. I think they're a whole lot of fun, and as you can see from me and Kyle, they can actually save your life!"

9
Game, Sex & Match

Sexual play isn't just fun: It can make all the difference between a happy and creative sex life and a sex life that's dogged by frustration and misunderstanding. You can use sexual play not only to show your partner how much you love him, but more than that; you can use it to show him how to *return* your love. Through role-playing and playful behavior, you can teach him how to excite you and please you in all the ways you like best.

Like all games, good sexual play depends on understanding, intuition, imagination, and skill—as well as a totally positive frame of mind. In the previous chapter, Sue-Ann brought a positive frame of mind to bear on her husband's impotence, and cured it. That same positive frame of mind can work wonders for *your* sexual relationships, too.

You should be not only positive, but light-hearted. Never be afraid to laugh when you're having sex. Never be afraid to try anything just because it might look ridiculous. If you were an alien and you came across two humans having sexual intercourse without having any knowledge of love or passion or the strength of our physical urges, you'd think that what they were doing was absurd. No wonder the aliens in *The X-Files* are always abducting people and giving them a thorough sexual examination.

Of course sex isn't absurd, but we should never become humorless and self-important in any of our relationships, particularly our sexual relationships, because that causes misunderstanding, antagonism and resentment. Try to cultivate a sense of humor, especially in bed.

Sexual play encompasses every sexual activity from rolling around in the rain to the sophisticated extremes of sado-masochism. Only you know what secretly turns you on, but sexual play will enable you, perhaps for the very first time, to share it with your partner.

Make sure you get what you need out of sexual play, but at the same time don't be selfish. You may not particularly care for your partner's taste in sexual stimulation, but sexual play is all about give and take.

To show you just how varied sexual play can be, here's one of the most memorable erotic games

I came across while I was researching this book, plus a few more suggestions for sex games of your own.

Sheila, 23, a jeweler from Scottsdale, Arizona: "My boyfriend Ray and I were always having arguments. Not serious arguments, just nagging each other and putting each other down. I don't know why. I guess maybe we were testing each other, needling each other, trying to provoke some kind of response. Our relationship wasn't bad, you know, but it had gotten pretty routine. I wouldn't say that the fire had gone out, but it wasn't exactly a raging inferno.

"Last Valentine's Day I made Ray a special dinner. Chili, which his his favorite, with salad and rice and tortillas; and then a Key Lime Pie because he was always saying how much he loved Key Lime Pie. And whipped cream in a can, because he loved to squirt heaps and heaps of it on top of his desserts.

"He came around and he had forgotten that it was Valentine's Day. I don't know how anybody can possibly forget that it's Valentine's Day, with all the cards in the shops and all the advertising on TV, but Ray managed it. I had a card for him and some aftershave and everything, and he didn't even bring me so much as a single dead flower.

"Well, I was so angry. I was *hurt*! I'd bought myself a new red top, with a deep scoop neck, and a little white skirt to go with it, and some red lace panties. I'd really made an effort to be romantic and show him that I loved him, and what did I get in return? 'Oh, sorry.' That was it. 'Oh, sorry.'

"We sat down at the table and I served up some chili. Ray took a mouthful and said, 'Hmm, this is good. But you needn't have gone to all this trouble. I was going to take you out for a pizza.' That was it. I snapped. He was just helping himself to salad and I said, 'You want Thousand Island dressing with your salad? Or don't you think I should have gone to all that trouble?' And I poured all the dressing over his head.

"He raked his fingers through his hair and looked at all this dressing in his hands. Then he went ape. He reached over and grabbed hold of my breasts, leaving Thousand Island fingermarks all over my new top. I picked a handful of salad out of the bowl and crammed it down the front of his T-shirt. So he took a spoonful of chili and flicked it all over me, all over my face, all over my hair, all over my new white shorts. I took the jug of fruit punch and poured it into his lap, ice-cubes, orange slices, mint leaves, and everything.

"I said, 'Get out of here! You're crazy! Look at my shorts!' I had to soak my shorts in cold water, otherwise the chili was going to leave a stain. I got up and went to the laundry room and took off my shorts. But Ray followed me and came right up behind me.

"I said, 'I told you! Get out of here! I never want to see you again!'

"He said, 'Can't I just butter you up a little?'

"I didn't see it coming. I said, 'You can butter me up all you want but it won't do you any good.'

"As soon as I said that, he pulled out my pantie-elastic and thrust his hand right down the front of them, and his hand was filled with soft-spread margarine. He pushed it right into my pussy and wiped his fingers on my stomach.

"I was screaming. I chased him back into the breakfast room and caught him as he tried to dodge around the table. He lost his balance and fell back on the couch. I dragged down his track-suit pants and his jockey shorts and I took the Key Lime Pie from the table and I squashed it all over his cock and his balls, and squidged it right in. I was just about to add some whipped cream but he managed to grab my waist and force me over onto my back. He lifted up my top and started to squirt cream all over my breasts, starting with my nipples, and making huge piles of it on each breast.

"By this time, we were both laughing so much that we couldn't breathe. I managed to twist the cream can around and squirt some into Ray's face. He squirted a whole pile of into my face, too, so that I was coughing and spluttering. Then he held me down, and took a handful of cherry tomatoes from the table and started to push them into my asshole, one by one. I was struggling like a wildcat but Ray's very strong and my asshole was all slippery with margarine, so it couldn't have been difficult. I don't know many he got up there, maybe six or seven.

"Then he held me down and we looked into each other's eyes and both of us were smiling and both of us knew that we were in love. I guess that was what we hadn't been able to say to each other. We'd both been looking for commitment, but neither of us had been prepared to be the first one to admit that they wanted to give it.

"I reached down and Ray's cock was hard and sticky and covered in Key Lime Pie. I massaged it and it was deliciously hard. I tugged my panties to one side, and I took his cock and pressed it up against my buttery pussy. 'I want it in all the way,' I told him, and when I said 'all the way' he knew what I meant.

"We had the messiest fuck ever. Ray's hands kept squeezing my cream-covered breasts, and there were crumbs everywhere. But I had an orgasm that made me want to hold Ray so close to me that we could never be seperated, even though his hair was smothered in salad dressing. He took himself out of me before he climaxed, because he hadn't used a condom, and I rubbed that Key Lime-y cock until he shot out a whole load of warm sperm, all over by breasts and my stomach.

"I said, 'I didn't ask for extra cream, did I?' But he didn't say anything. He just kissed me and wouldn't stop kissing me and I knew then that everything was going to be so much better."

You, too, could try an erotic food fight. Or else you might like to try one of these:

Shipwrecked Mariners: You and your partner have been shipwrecked on your bed, which is your desert island. You have no clothes except for what you can improvize out of two handkerchiefs. You are allowed to swim to a neighboring island (the kitchen) for supplies, but you must eat and drink only what you would normally find on a desert island—fruit, nuts, and water. No Cheez Whiz, and crackers is cheating. You can't watch television, you mustn't listen to music. You must make your own entertainment. You are only rescued when you have both had three climaxes.

Tattoo Artists: Using colored felt-tip pens, you decorate each other's naked bodies with elaborate and exotic patterns. You should take your time over this, particularly when it comes to drawing your "tattooes" on breasts and genitals.

Nude Housekeeper: Of course, nude male housekeepers are actually available for those women who are prepared to pay for them. But your partner can do just as good a job. He must spend a whole day completely naked doing whatever you ask him to do: cleaning, cooking, bathing you, dressing you. You can degrade him as much as you like (using his tongue for toilet tissue, for example.) He must submit to absolutely anything and everything you want him to do. He is not allowed to question any of your instructions, and any reluctance or refusal will result in a punishment of your choosing (such as having seven pubic hairs pulled out.) Men who have a masochistic streak will adore this game. Less submissive men can look forward to a future scenario in which *you* play the part of the nude housekeeper, and have to do everything that *he* commands.

Statues: One of you is a statue, unable to move, unable to speak. The other is a great admirer of statuary, and caresses and fondles the statue in admiration. This is a game of bondage without the ropes and the handcuffs, and depends entirely on the statue to remain motionless while the sculpture lover does just that ... makes love to the sculpture. This game can be incredibly sensual, particularly if you use massage oils or other perfumed lubricants, and play it in an atmosphere of warmth and calm. The statue can only be brought to life by experiencing a sexual orgasm.

Blind Woman's Bluff: Naked, you allow your partner to blindfold you. Then you must guess what he is touching or caressing you with, between your legs. An ostrich feather, maybe, or a paintbrush, or half a mango fruit. As the game progresses, he can insert various (safe) objects into your vagina for you to identify. Bananas, pickles, suckers, popsicles. Finally, an erect penis.

Wrestlers: Start this game with a ritual shaving

of each other's body hair, with plenty of perfumed soap and fresh blades, until you are both completely depilated. (If your partner is exceptionally hairy, don't bother. Play King Kong instead.) Once shaved, put down a blanket on the floor and then cover each other all over with baby oil, paying special attention to your sensitive areas. Tie a single strand of yarn around your partner's penis, and insert a similar strand in your vagina so that only an inch of it shows. The winner is whichever of you manages to capture your partner's strand of wool. No pinching, biting or scratching. But according to Linda, a 25-year-old model from Seattle, Washington, who told me about it: "It's easily the sexiest thing that two people can do together. If you're not making love before the end of round one, I'll be amazed."

The sexual games you play with your partner are limitless. They allow you to be whoever you want and to do whatever you want—to shed your inhibitions like a butterfly emerging from its chrysalis, and fly.

Enjoy your games. Enjoy your partner's affection. And most of all, enjoy the God-given gifts of laughter and love.

PENGUIN PUTNAM INC.
Online

Your Internet gateway to a virtual environment with
hundreds of entertaining and enlightening books from
Penguin Putnam Inc.

*While you're there, get the latest buzz on
the best authors and books around—*

Tom Clancy, Patricia Cornwell, W.E.B. Griffin,
Nora Roberts, William Gibson, Robin Cook,
Brian Jacques, Catherine Coulter, Stephen King,
Jacquelyn Mitchard, and many more!

**Penguin Putnam Online is located at
http://www.penguinputnam.com**

PENGUIN PUTNAM NEWS

Every month you'll get an inside look at our upcoming
books and new features on our site. This is an ongoing
effort to provide you with the most up-to-date
information about our books and authors.

Subscribe to Penguin Putnam News at
http://www.penguinputnam.com/ClubPPI